Basic Illustrated Guide

For Microsoft Word

by C. Allan Butkus

This book is dedicated to those who have something to say.

Although we all had ancestors 200 years ago, we know little or nothing of their lives.

When we are gone, as we surely will, our memories, hopes, experiences, adventures, and dreams go with us.

Unless we leave our record. We are each unique.

"I realize I didn't do the job as well as you, but I did it to the best of my ability."
Reputed to Thomas Jefferson

Table Of Contents

Introduction

This book is not written for idiots or dummies and it is not written for or by a computer guru. The purpose of this book is to help you become a better writer. In essence, this book is a graphic toolbox. It is written for the person who has something to say, but is not certain of how to approach the process. This book has been created to help you understand and master the mechanics of transferring ideas from your mind to paper

There are no prerequisites.

Fear not the unknown. This book will feed you the information you need, when you need it. It is a basic graphic guide to using the computer to write. There is a section for those of you who need it, on what type of equipment to purchase. Another section, provides definitions of this new language, with illustrations. I believe you will be pleasantly surprised when you find out how easy it is to enter this new world.

Obviously, the best way to learn is to have someone show us by standing at our side. If you can find someone to help you, please do. In days long past, complicated skills were learned by apprenticeship. But times have changed and we must change with them.

This book is the next best thing to having a computer geek standing at your side.

You are about to learn a new language. The language of the computer. It may seem complicated and it is. Nevertheless, it is comprehensible and it not nearly as complicated as some of the things you've had to learn. Such as dealing with the opposite sex.
Remember, **Everyone, in all new endeavors <u>always</u> begins as an amateur.**

As we begin, ask yourself this question

Are you ready to become a more effective writer?
If the answer is yes, read the following statement.
I am a writer and I know it.
Read it aloud.
Read it aloud again.
If you truly believe this, put the words down on paper. Use a piece of paper and pencil.
That wasn't so hard was it?
You are now a writer.

And now is the time to begin evolving. For writers are not born – **<u>They Evolve</u>**.

Do you need a computer to write a book? No, you don't. Many books have been written using quills and parchment, pencils and paper, and eventually the typewriter. Why were these changes made? Because a better way exists.

The computer eliminated the typewriter because it is more powerful. A computer can be thought of as a typewriter on steroids. One of its most important characteristics is that it remembers. It also has the capability of spellchecking, printing words, sentences, paragraphs, and chapters, and it can store the information and print it in different formats. Whole sections of the book can be repositioned using very little effort. All of this power is at your fingertips.

The computer is not some demonic creation which has been complicated beyond all understanding. It is technology, it is an electronic machine. But above all, it is a tool. A tool you can and will learn to use. For technology is the servant of mankind.

However, the fundamentals of machines must be learned.

No one in the history of the world has ever been able to understand the capabilities of a computer without first being taught.

There is a progression which takes place in learning anything new. It is necessary to learn how to add before you can subtract. The multiplication tables need to be understood before it is possible to understand division. The same applies to computers. As we learn, we build upon what we know.

Learning is an innate human trait. We crawl before we learn to walk, we may fall repeatedly as we learn, but we do learn. Because we get up after each fall.

Writing effectively is an acquired skill. A learned skill. The mechanics of writing are much easier to understand when the information is presented clearly.

There are many different reasons to write. Each of us has had experiences no one else has ever had. When you are gone your memories will go with you. But by writing, you can leave a record that you existed, that you had value, and what you thought. Unfortunately, most people are looking ahead and forgetting the lessons of history. Although the future is a challenge, much can be learned by simply looking behind us. What you want to write and the reasons that you want to write are yours to explore. This book will help you find a way to get the words from your head to paper.

Learning is an extremely personal process. As a person, you will grow as you learn.

> *'All the words I use in my stories can be found in the dictionary — it's just a matter of arranging them into the right sentences.'*　　*W. Somerset Maugham*

Writing is an evolving skill. The longer you do it, and the harder you try, the better you will get. You can't buy the creation of your story. You are the one who must nurture it and give it birth. You are the one to breathe life into your work.

The emotion you will experience when you hold your completed book in your hand, is a proud moment. For this is your book.

More than a century ago, Henry Ford said:

'If you believe you can or you can't, you're right.'

What do we have to work with?

Microsoft Word is powerful program with many capabilities There have been many versions since its inception in in 1983.

Version 2016 is a current version which works with Windows 7 and 8.1, as well as Windows 10. It is possible to purchase this version outright, without any additional subscription charges. Currently, it is not expensive.

Version 2019 is also a current version but it only works with Windows 10. It is possible to purchase this version outright, without any additional subscription charges.

Office 365 is also current, but there is a monthly charge for its use. The advantage of this model is that you will constantly be using the most current version. The disadvantage, you will always be paying for it.

Technology changes rapidly and new versions of software are constantly appearing. This does not mean that the older versions do not fulfill the needs of the user. It does mean, that the newer version will have more capabilities. It is up to you as the user to decide how much is enough.

This book is written using Microsoft Word 2016, and Widows 7. Windows 10 will have a homepage different from Windows 7. What is important is the functioning of the word processing program and that will be the same.

Word 2016, 2019 and office 365 are quite similar. There are differences, but none that should affect the new writer.

This book is divided up into different segments. **It does not have to be read in any specific order.**

There is a section on choosing equipment, but if you already have a computer, a quick review of the section will be sufficient.

There is a reference section titled Definitions. When you run across a phase and need to clarify it, this is a good place to try some one-stop shopping. Definitions are given as well as graphics. Sometimes it's simpler to understand something if you can see a picture of it

The heart of this book is the section referred to as Snippets. Here you will find detailed screen by screen instructions with graphics which detail how to get the most from your computer. Each of the topics covered in this section follow a standard format.

In many instances there is a fundamental error when technical information is presented. In the traditional method, the teacher or instructor explains to the student How something works. The student, on the other hand first needs to know What it is that this thing does and then the Why. The final step for the learner is the How. Therefore, in each Snippet presented the format; What, Why, and the How are presented before each explanation.

As your knowledge of writing increases, so will your need for the information contained in the Snippets. **Learn the basics of how to get the words from your head to the computer monitor and then to paper.** <u>This is the important part.</u> The Snippets will help you later when you need them.

How does all this work?

You have an idea for a story. You need some way of getting the idea from your head onto a sheet of paper.

You type your story on the keyboard, it appears on a monitor, you print it, and then save it. That's all there is to it.

You may wonder why you need to save your work. The reason is simple, your work has value.

By saving your work, you can later manipulate it. As you work, your ideas will grow and change. You have the ability to give them life. As the writer, you control the ideas you are conveying to the reader.

Major Considerations

There is no best computer for everyone. The computer is a tool and for it to be effective it must fit your individual needs.

Factors to consider:

1) Reliability
2) Cost
3) Physical size
4) Capability

1) **Reliability** is the most important consideration when choosing a computer or other equipment. <u>Technology is a servant of mankind</u>. It must function as intended. Your words, your thoughts, your creative endeavors can be distorted or lost if your equipment is not reliable. Ideas are elusive and they can escape and be forever gone in less than a heartbeat. Never to be recalled. Fortunately, most computer systems which use quality components are reliable. Do not buy equipment exclusively on price.

2) **The Cost of Equipment** is frequently driven by innovation. The newest stuff costs the most. This does not mean that older technology doesn't function well. It only means that there is newer technology which offers additional features. Technology which is cutting edge today, will in one year be outdated. What does this mean to you? Buy equipment which fulfills your needs **today** but continue to watch for innovations.

3) **Physical Size**   Where and how you write will determine what equipment you need. If space is not a consideration, a desktop computer is a good choice. If you plan to take the computer with you when you travel, a laptop is the best choice. Or you may choose to buy both. Assure that the operating systems are compatible (Do they both work on the same version of Windows? Do they both work on the same version of Word?) If you don't know ask.

4) **The Capability** of the equipment is a prime consideration. Can the equipment satisfy your needs? Is operating speed adequate? Is noise a consideration? Size? Appearance?

How to Write on a Computer

When you purchase your computer be certain to have **Microsoft Word 2016** installed. (If you use a different version of Microsoft Word there may be variations, which will affect the following graphics.)

An icon on your computer desktop will identify where the program is located.

Special note: Your home screen will differ from my home screen.
The important part of looking at this screen is the Microsoft Word Icon.

Turn the computer on.
The background on your monitor is called wallpaper. It is not as important as the small pictures (called icons) on the screen. These icons are the keys to moving from place to place on the computer. This is referred to as navigating on the monitor of the computer.

When the computer has completed its startup procedures the Home Screen will be displayed

Using your mouse, point at the icon for your **Word 2016** and single left-click

The **Word 2016 icon** will light up.   (This identifies the program)
Then double-left click on it again.   (This tells the computer to open the program)

Screen will change

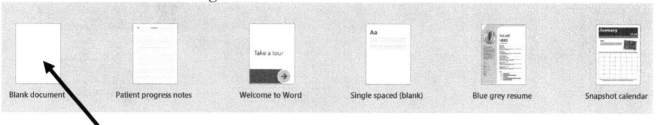

Single left-click on blank document
The screen will change, and display the **Home Screen for Word 2016**

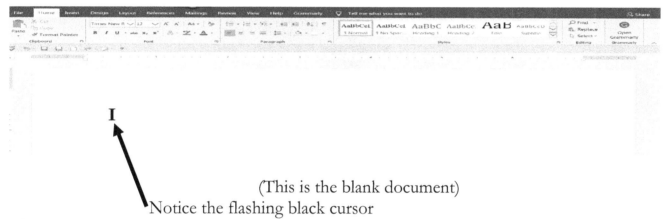

(This is the blank document)
Notice the flashing black cursor
This is the location where your text will begin to be displayed.

As you type on the keyboard, the characters will appear on the screen.
        Congratulations! You have taken a major step in mastering the computer.
When your document is complete, print it.

Special note: (Computers are powerful and they also allow the use of Speech Recognition Software. Using this technology, it is possible to speak into a microphone and have the words automatically typed on the screen. A major advantage of this type of this technology is that the computer will type words, you can pronounce, but not spell. Additionally, it is not necessary to be a fast typist.
This technology allows you to get ideas into the computer before they can escape.
        Examples include:
                Dragon NaturallySpeaking
                Tatzi
                Voice Finger

Printing Your Document

This is done by choosing **File** on the monitor's **Menu bar.**

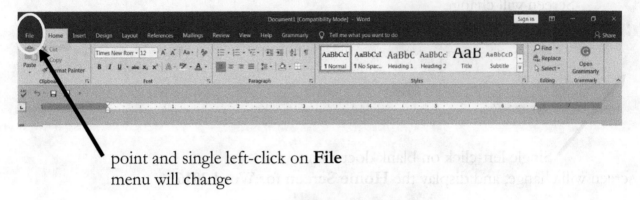

point and single left-click on **File**
menu will change

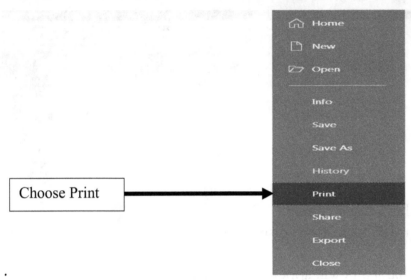

Choose Print ➡

menu will change

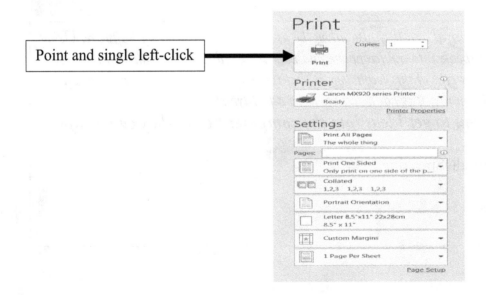

Point and single left-click ➡

The document will print

Saving your Document

Now comes the most important part of the process. Saving the document. This is also done by pointing and clicking.

Point at **File** and single left-click

Menu will change

Point and single left-click on **Save**

Point in single left click on **Browse**

menu will change
Documents library

Type in the name of the file you're saving.

Point and single left-click on **Save**

Your document has now been saved.

Realize What You Have Done

You input text to a word processing program.

You have a hard copy (printed copy).

You saved a copy (electronic copy), which you can retrieve later and edit or modify it, if needed.

Congratulations! You are on your way to become a more effective writer.

Choosing Equipment

Your lifestyle and writing patterns will dictate the type of equipment you will want and what you need. Do not handicap yourself with inferior equipment. Although you can't buy your way into being an award-winning author, you can inhibit the possibility of that happening. Purchase equipment adequate for your needs. A $5000 gaming computer and monstrous monitor will tell your story no more effectively than a $200 desktop computer.

What do you need? **A computer system and a printer.**

Selecting equipment does not have to be a terrifying experience.
Your needs are basic:
A method of transferring your thoughts to a place where they can be manipulated. This is usually accomplished using a computer. Next, you will need a method of moving your thoughts from the computer to paper. This is done with a printer.

The computer: There are two popular choices:

The desktop computer system is the primary choice for many. They are usually more economical and powerful. They are not self-contained, and require household electrical current. They are composed of four parts:

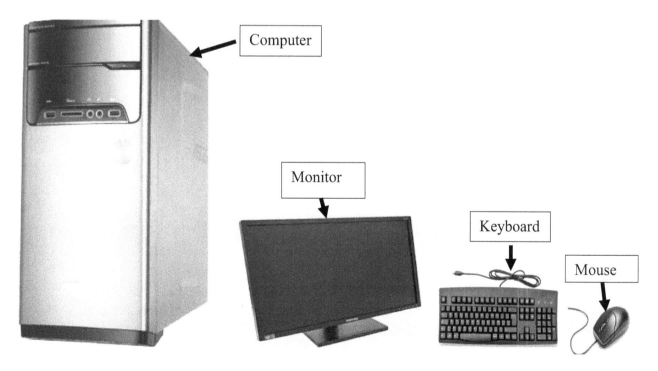

Computer

Monitor

Keyboard

Mouse

It will have more USB ports and they will be located on the **front and rear** of the computer. (These ports are quick connect locations for additional equipment.)

They will also have additional internal card slots, and the capability of expanding storage capability (both RAM, SSD, and additional hard drives).

They are more physically stable. Less prone to damage from movement and use a separate keyboard. If the keyboard is damaged, a new one can be purchased for approximately $20. If the keyboard on a laptop goes out, you buy a new laptop.

Larger monitors available which improve the ability to review text and graphics. There is the option available to use different pointing devices. It is possible to use a mouse, trackball, or touchpad. (It is also possible to use these on a laptop, but they are not as conveniently connected.)

Other considerations

Physical size and weight, which will vary by model and features desired. Consequently, space constraints may be critical.

The laptop computer also has valuable characteristics. It has the advantage of being self-contained, portable, and convenient to use. They can be powered by batteries or by plugging into a household electrical circuit.

A disadvantage is it usually operates slower than a desktop machine and has limited expansion capabilities. The screens are smaller. They are usually more costly. A major disadvantage is they do not bounce well. When using a word processor for writing, speed is usually not a critical factor.

Convenience.
Prestige.
They are usually lightweight and portable.
Everything is contained in one unit, except for the printer.
Usually only one or two USB ports
There are a few wires to connect.
They usually contain a camera (This can be an advantage or disadvantage).
Some models have detachable screens or screens which can be reversed. This is a valuable function for making presentations.

Other considerations

Cost. More expensive than a desktop computer with the same capabilities.
If anything breaks on malfunctions, the unit becomes inoperative.
Repairs are expensive.
Care must be taken during transport. They are fragile.
Significant danger of theft. Readily marketable.
Many are relatively heavy for their size.

Software

A computer is hardware, the way that it talks to itself, is by using software (pre-programmed instructions telling the computer what to do, in an electronic digital language the computer understands.)

Example of software

Computers are not smart, but they are fast and follow directions. As of this writing, most computers will be using an operating system (software) called Windows. It will most probably be installed on your computer when you purchase it. Next, you will need a computer program (software) which allows you to tell the computer what you want to it to do. One of the most popular programs writers use today is a word processing program called **Word**. It is part of a package of programs from Microsoft named **Office**. The information contained in this book will be based on **Word 2016. There are newer versions of Word, but this version was chosen because there are no annual fees charged for use of the program.** It is easily installed on either a laptop or desktop computer. Many of these instructions are compatible with older versions of **Word,** but there may be slight variations. The essence of the instructions will be the same.

Printers

The two most popular choices are **Inkjet** printers, and **Laser** printers. Both are electromechanical devices (a blend of electronic and mechanical).

<u>An important consideration when choosing a printer is its operating cost.</u>

Inkjet printers use ink in the printing process. The ink is extremely expensive. (Generic ink tanks are available but care must be taken to assure quality. Poor quality ink can destroy a quality Inkjet printer). If you purchase generic ink, assure that it meets the standards for **ISO 9001**. This is an international quality measurement standard, and will be listed in the specifications for the ink. The difference in cost is significant. Manufacturers ink is frequently 15 times higher than generic ink.

Machines which use <u>individual</u> color ink tanks are more economical. When a color runs out you only replace the depleted color. Replacement is simple. Printing speed is adequate.

Laser printers print use a heat (thermal) process and do not use ink, they use toner (a dry powdered substance). Many laser printers are significantly more economical (although initial cost may be higher) to operate than inkjet printers and they operate much faster. Some models print about a page a second. Many can print 30,000 to 60,000 pages before the toner needs to be replaced. Toner replacement is quite simple

Special note:

Do not buy a printer only because of price. Many manufacturers offer printers at a low price because they will charge more for the ink or toner. Because of this, frequently it is cheaper to buy another printer than to buy ink.

If the printer is only to be used for writing, the black ink will be depleted faster than the other colors. It is wise to purchase a printer where the black ink can be replaced separately.

Laser printers can be purchased which print in color or only in black.

Those printers which print only in black (mono tone) are usually less expensive, but not significantly so.

Some printers (both ink jet and laser) have a useful feature called **Duplex printing**. This means it will print on both sides of a sheet of paper. <u>This is a valuable feature.</u>

Buy with quality and reliability in mind. You should not have to worry about your printer.

Pointing Devices

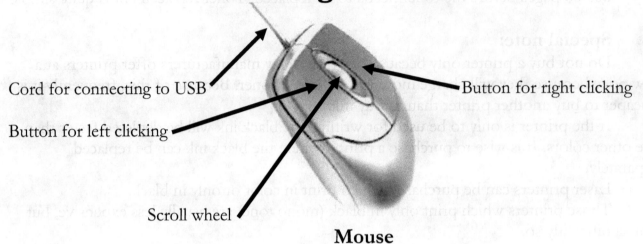

Cord for connecting to USB

Button for left clicking

Scroll wheel

Button for right clicking

Mouse

What: In computer technology, a mouse is a pointing device.
It is used to move the cursor on the screen of the monitor in order to select various options. This is called scrolling.

Although there are many different types of these devices, they are quite similar. Battery powered cordless versions are quite popular and function well.

All will have options for moving
  1) cursor on the screen
  2) left clicking
  3) right clicking
  4) upward and downward scrolling.

> **Special note**: *When the control key* **v** *is held down, and the scroll wheel is rotated, it will increase or decrease the size of the image on the screen.*

Why: Pointing devices enable the computer user to communicate to the computer what functions are to be performed.

How: Physically moving the mouse in any direction will move the cursor on the screen.

A single left-click **will highlight** an item on the monitor screen.

Double left-clicking **will select** the item on the monitor screen.

A single right-click causes a **drop-down menu** to appear which allows other functions to be performed.

Moving the scrolling wheel up or down **will move the cursor** in that same direction.

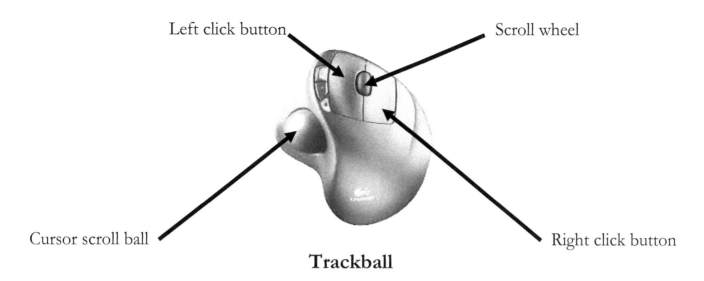

Left click button   Scroll wheel

Cursor scroll ball   Right click button

Trackball

What: In computer technology, a trackball is a pointing device. It is used to move the cursor on the screen of the monitor in order to select various options. **It does not have to be physically moved on the desktop to move the cursor.** Rotating the Cursor scroll ball changes the position of the cursor.

Although there are many different types of these devices, they are quite similar. Battery powered cordless versions are quite popular and function well.

All will have options for:
1) moving cursor on the screen
2) left clicking
3) right clicking
4) upward and downward scrolling.

> **Special note**: *When the control key* **v** *is held down, and the scroll wheel is rotated, it will increase or decrease the size of the image on the screen.*

Why: Pointing devices enable the computer user to communicate to the computer what functions are to be performed.

How: The cursor is moved by **rotating the ball** with the thumb

A single left-click **will highlight** an item on the monitor screen.

Double left-clicking **will select** the item on the monitor screen.

A single right-click causes a **drop-down menu** to appear which allows other functions to be performed.
Moving the scrolling wheel up or down will move the cursor in that same direction.

Touchpads

Special note: Some laptop computers have a special touchpad on their keyboards for moving the cursor on the screen. The functions of the mouse are performed by moving your finger across the touchpad. These features vary by manufacturer.

Definitions

Backspace Key

Is used to delete the text character to the left of the cursor.

Central Processor Unit (CPU)

Hardware component. This is the brain of the computer. It controls what and when. Originally each CPU had one brain, which is sufficient for word processing.

Most computers now use quad (4) processors and some state-of-the-art CPUs use 32 processors.

CD/DVD Drive

A electromechanical device for manipulating data. Similar to a small turntable.

Compact Disc drive is unit which plays a small plastic disc (4.7 inch/120 MM) on which digital information is stored. It is read using reflected laser light.

Digital Video Disc is unit which plays a small plastic disc (4.7 inch/120 MM) which holds significantly more data than a CD. It is read using reflected laser light.

Technology is rapidly advancing using Blu-ray and archival storage. This latter technology allows the storage of approximately 65,000,000 pages of text on one disc.

23

Chip	Generic term for hardware in the computer.

Composed of integrated circuits. Usually a device which can be plugged in to provide additional capabilities.

Cloud Memory Storage	Is a method of saving your files, but not on your computer. The data that you create is stored in another location, usually on someone else's computer. Many believe this is a beneficial service. There may be a charge for the service.

Computer	An electronic device for storing and processing data. They are machines which have few moving parts. They function by using software.

or

Computer Speed	Refers to how fast your computer can do what you request. Most modern machines operate at speeds of 3.0 to 4.0 GHz per second. (This equates to 3 billion to 4 billion cycles per second).

Information: The more cores a CPU contains, the faster it can process complex data. Usually, word processing does not require massive CPUs or ultra-speed computing.

Cursor	Usually a flashing black line (I) on the screen. It is a movable indicator which is controlled by a mouse or other pointing indicator. It determines where data will be inserted. It is possible to change the appearance of the cursor.

Cut and Paste	Used to manipulate text. Text is highlighted first and then it can be; 1) copied to be used elsewhere, 2) removed from its current position, 3) inserted in a different position. (See Snippets Highlighting)
Default Settings	Refers to the preset values in a program. These are the basic settings and can be changed to become more user-friendly. (See Snippets Default Settings)
Delete Key	Is used to delete the character to the right of the cursor, or other highlighted information.

Digital Language	A language composed of ones and zeros. Different programs group these two values into words of different lengths in order to process information more efficiently. *Example: 0001 0010 0011 equates to 1 2 3*
Enter Key	Is used to send the cursor to the next line or execute a command or operation.

Most full-sized PC keyboards have two Enter keys; one above the right Shift key and another on the bottom right of the Numeric keypad.

Flash Drive	Hardware component.

A portable method of storing data and transferring it. They are available in different formats; USB stick, SD memory cards, Thumb Drive etc.

Floppy Drive	Old technology. A method of inserting information into a computer using a removable disk.

They have been replaced in modern computers by CD/DVD drives, and flash drives.

Font	Basically, text characters using different forms of letters. Examples: ABC, *ABC*, ABC. A graphical representation of text in a different typeface, Microsoft Word offers a vast selection of fonts. Others can be added.

Hard Disk Drive (HHD)	A hardware component in the computer that stores data.

Data in memory is retained even when power is off. The data is stored in concentric rings. Operates similar to a record turntable. Older technology.

Highlighting	Is a method of selecting text by using a pointing device. (Examples: A mouse, trackball, touchpad, or touchscreen) This is done by clicking on the item to be highlighted. The color of the item will change. *Example: Now is the time for all good men* (see Snippets Highlighting)

Homepage Microsoft Word	The introductory page which typically serves as a starting place and table of contents for the site.

Icon	A small picture on your monitor which represents an activation link to a computer program or other function.

Example:

Inkjet Printer	Hardware component.

An electromechanical machine which uses ink to print on paper. Most use a water-soluble ink, but some use pigment-based ink.

Laptop Computer	Is a battery or AC-powered personal computer.

Usually smaller than a briefcase that can easily be transported and conveniently used in temporary spaces such as on airplanes, in libraries, temporary offices, and at meetings.

Laser Printer   Hardware component.

An electromechanical machine which uses a thermal process to print on paper. Will print in black and white or color. Toner is a powder which is electrically bonded to paper using a thermal process. It is not water soluble.

Line Spacing   The vertical distance between lines of text in the document.

Margin   In word processing, it is the space between the text and the edge of your document.
(See snippets   Standard Document Format)

Menu   A menu is a set of options presented to the user in a graphic form. Their function is similar to a menu in a restaurant. Its purpose is to help the user find relevant information and functions related to the current process.

Menu Bar   Located at the top of your document in Microsoft Word. It only contains words (tabs) which open up access to toolbars

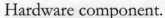

Mouse	In computer technology, a mouse is a pointing device.

For additional information see **Mouse** in the section.
(see Snippets   Pointing Devices)

Paragraph	A section of text dealing with a particular idea, usually dealing with a single theme and indicated by a new line, indentation, or numbering.
Peripheral	There are many different peripheral devices, but they fall into three general categories:

  Input devices, such as a mouse or keyboard.
  Output devices, such as the monitor or a printer.
  Storage devices, such as a hard drive or flash drive.

Quick Access Toolbar	Is located below the toolbar of Microsoft Word.

It contains icons for often used functions. It is possible to add and remove commands with relative ease. Extremely valuable feature.
(see Snippets   Quick Access Toolbar)

RAM   Random Access Memory

Hardware chip in a computer for temporarily storing information.

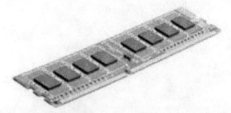

This is the working memory of the computer. When the computer is turned off, it loses stored information. In most cases more RAM increases computer speed. For most word processing operations 4 Gb of RAM are sufficient, *(Information: at 200 words per page, 1 Gb equals approximately 130,000 pages of text.)*

Software

Is a set of pre-programmed instructions telling the computer what to do. It contains an electronic digital language the computer understands.
(Information: The following is an example of computer code.
 <p>If you input wrong value, the program will return
<samp>Error!</samp></p> ... The HTML **<code>**
element

Solid-State Drive (SSD)

A hardware component in a computer that stores data.

These may be installed in the computer or externally by cable. It is the current technology and is rapidly replacing conventional hard drives (HHD). Data in memory is retained even when power is off. It operates significantly faster than the conventional HHD. This is an important consideration when choosing a machine. Much more reliable than hard drive

Standard Document Format	Is the generally accepted standard for documents. Margins are set at 1 inch (2.54 cm) for upper and lower, as well as left and right. Recommended fonts are Times New Roman and Courier. The size of the font is 12. Line spacing is set to double. Indentation is .5 inches. (1.27 cm) (see Snippet Standard Document Format)
Tab Key	In many programs, an indent for the first line of text can be created by moving the cursor to the  beginning of the line and pressing the **Tab** key on the keyboard. In standard document format the indent is .5 inches. (1.27 cm)
Toolbars	Are located under the menu bar. They are accessed by single-left clicking on a specific tab. This opens the options related to the tab. 
Trackball	In computer technology, a trackball is a pointing device.  For additional information see **Trackball** in the section (see Snippets Pointing Devices)
Text	Text is usually composed of a font which conveys meaning to the person who examines it. The previous statement, as well as this, are examples of text.

USB port	Hardware component.

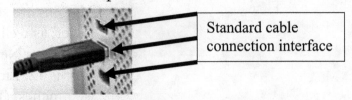

Universal **S**erial **B**us

Wallpaper	Is decorative background of a graphical nature on the screen of a computer monitor.
Word Processor	Is software which allows users to create, edit, and print documents. It enables the ability to write text, store it electronically, display it on a screen, modify it by entering commands and characters from the keyboard, and print it.

Note: Microsoft Word is the most widely used word processing program on the market and has different versions, with different capabilities. Microsoft Office 2016 and 2019 are standalone, local (not cloud-based, like Office 365). Each new release provides increased capabilities, but with increased cost. Many new word processing programs have a reoccurring cost.

Snippets

Alphabetical Listing

Some of these snippets provide more than one way of doing something. There is no need to master all methods. Determine which instruction works for you and use it. If you need to, make notations to aid you in understanding the different processes.

Learning is a journey. Enjoy the trip.

Backing up Files Using a CD or DVD

What: It is necessary to preserve the information which has been previously saved. It is recommended that your files be backed up at least every month. When the information is lost – it is permanently gone.

        If you only have one copy of your file   **It is not backed up**

        You will never get a warning that your files are going to be lost

        You do not have a guardian angel protecting your files

Why: This is referred to as <u>backing up your files.</u> Data and information loss can occur from a variety of causes; computer viruses, hardware failure, file corruption, fire, flood, or theft, etc.

There are different methods of backing up your files using; **CD/DVD, Flash Drive, External Hard Drive, SSD, or Cloud Storage.**

The backed-up files should be located in another physical location. If your computer is damaged or stolen your files are no longer available.

How: When files are backed up, they are electronically saved.

Discs are cheap insurance compared to lost work

In the lower left-hand corner of your desktop homepage is the Microsoft ball

Single left-click on it.

    menu will change

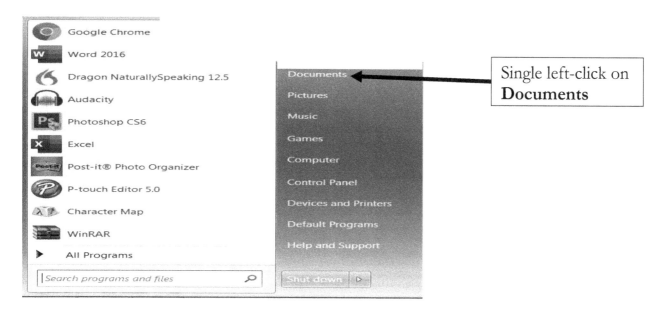

menu will change to **Documents Library**

You are now ready to identify which files you would like to save.

There are **two methods** to do this:

Using either of the **Shift Keys** on your keyboard.

Or the **Control Keys** on your keyboard.

Method One

A <u>quick method</u> of copying a **<u>range of files</u>** to be backed up is by using the **Shift Key**

    In the document library   single left-click on the first file to be saved.

    Identify last file to be copied and depress the shift key and simultaneously single left-click on the last file to be copied.

    The files which will be copied are now highlighted.

Method Two

This method allows the copying of **individual files**. This is useful when you wish to the copy specific files, but do not include files unrelated to your current project.

    In the Document Library single left-click on the first file to be saved. The file will be highlighted.

    Identify the next file to be saved and depress the **Control Key** as you single left-click on it.

    The file will be highlighted.

    Identify each subsequent file to be copied by depressing the **Control Key** and simultaneously single left-click on the last file to be copied.

    The files which will be copied are now highlighted.

After completing either of these two methods. The backup procedure remains the same.

Single left-click on the tab labeled **Burn**

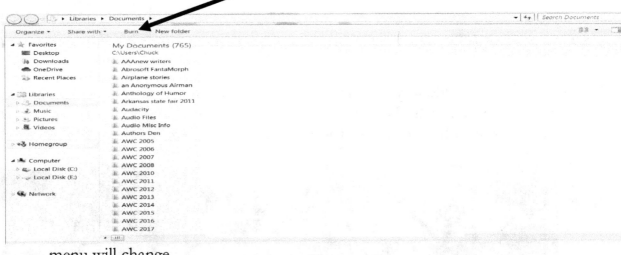

    menu will change

Press the button which opens your DVD/CD drive, on your computer.

    The computer will identify this location

        choose: Please insert a writable disc into drive D:

<u>Note: **Your computer may use another drive...**   **Choose the drive where DVD** will be inserted</u>

    menu will change

    to   **Burn a Disc (**and drive will open for DVD)

Insert an unused disc in drive D:

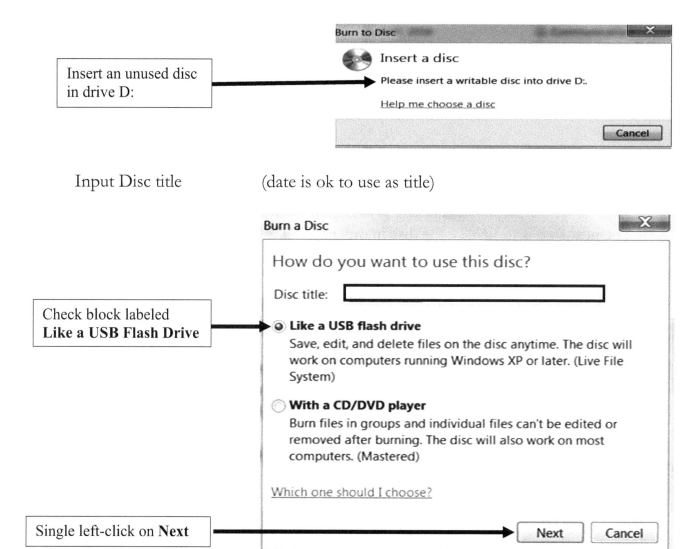

Burn to Disc

Insert a disc

Please insert a writable disc into drive D:.

Help me choose a disc

Cancel

Input Disc title   (date is ok to use as title)

Burn a Disc

How do you want to use this disc?

Disc title:

Check block labeled **Like a USB Flash Drive**

◉ **Like a USB flash drive**
Save, edit, and delete files on the disc anytime. The disc will work on computers running Windows XP or later. (Live File System)

◯ **With a CD/DVD player**
Burn files in groups and individual files can't be edited or removed after burning. The disc will also work on most computers. (Mastered)

Which one should I choose?

Single left-click on **Next**

Next   Cancel

menu will change to: **Formatting**

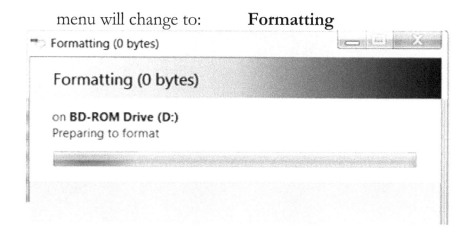

Formatting (0 bytes)

Formatting (0 bytes)

on **BD-ROM Drive (D:)**
Preparing to format

The formatting process readies the disk so that it can accept the files you are copying

When formatting of disc is completed   (this is an automatic process)
    Menu changes and files begin to be copied

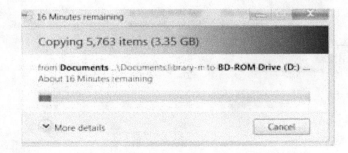

When copying is complete, menu will vanish
    Note: the speed of computer and number of files copied, determines how long copying takes
    The next step is to finalize the disc in order to use it later or in another machine

Press the button on the computer, which opens the drive door (the drive will not immediately open)
    The drive will run as it finalizes the copying and then open
        Using a permanent marker label the disc (by writing on the **top surface** of the disc.)
                Example: All words files   John Doe   8.3.2019
            Information: your files are written to the bottom of the disc

It is wise to create a second copy of your backed-up files periodically, if they are valuable and store it in <u>another physical location</u>. (In case of fire, theft, vandalism, or natural disaster)

    Once files are lost, they are gone forever.

Backing up files externally

USB Flash Drive
External Hard Drive.
Cloud Storage.

The methods of selecting files, is similar to the procedure using CD/DVD.
However, the actual transferring of files differs.

When using a flash drive, external hard drive, or cloud storage, it is first necessary to determine where that external source is located in the computer. This is easily done.

In the lower left-hand corner of your desktop homepage is the Microsoft ball

Single left-click on it.
    A new menu will appear
Single left-click on **Computer**

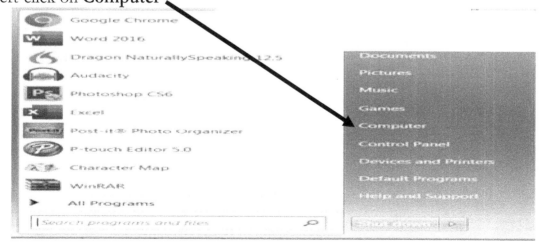

menu will appear listing the drives on your computer.

Install your external storage device in any available USB port on your computer. The new devices location will appear in the new menu

In this instance, it is identified as **K** [   ]

Note: the drive number may be different on your computer

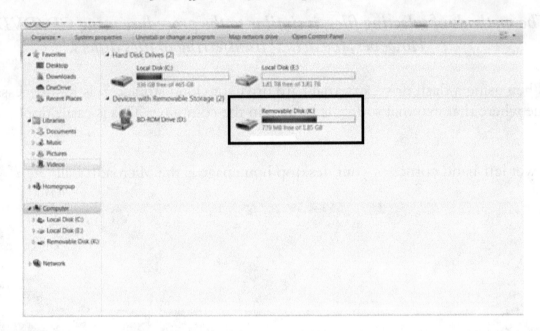

At this point, the external drive's location is known.

How to save files

In the lower left-hand corner of your desktop homepage is the Microsoft ball

Single left-click on it.

menu will change

Single left-click on **Documents**

Menu will change to **Documents Library**

You are now ready to identify which files you would like to save.

    There are **two methods** to do this:

        Using either of the **Shift Keys** on your keyboard.

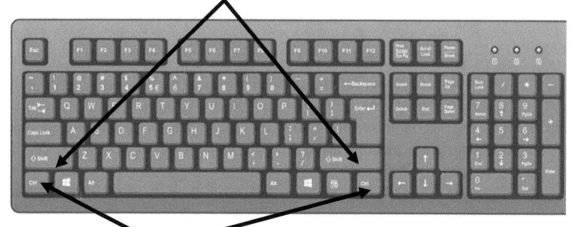

Or the **Control Keys** on your keyboard.

Method One

A quick method of copying a <u>range of files</u> to be backed up is by using the **Shift Key**
    In the document library   single left-click on the first file to be saved.
    Identify last file to be copied and depress the shift key and simultaneously single left-click on the last file to be copied.
        The files which will be copied are now highlighted.

Method Two

This method allows the copying of <u>individual files</u>. This is useful when you wish to copy specific files, but do not include files unrelated to your current project.

    In the **Document Library**   single left-click on the first file to be saved. The file will be highlighted.
    Identify the next file to be saved and depress the **Control Key** and single left-click on it.
        The file will be highlighted.
<u>Identify each subsequent file</u> to be copied by depressing the **Control Key** and simultaneously single left-click on the file to be copied.
        Each of the highlighted files will be copied.

You have now identified the files you wish to be backed up (by either method)
    There are two different ways to save files to the external drive.
        Method A   Drag-and-Drop
        Method B   Right Click Menu Method

Method A   Drag-And-Drop
        Place the cursor in the highlighted area of the files to be transferred

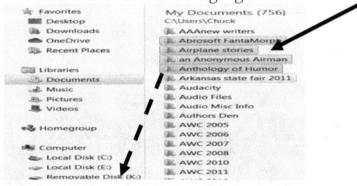

Left-click and hold the button down as you drag the cursor across the screen using the mouse to the location of your external drive.

    Release the left-click   the files will now be saved on the external drive.

Method B   Using Right-Click Menus.

Place the cursor in the highlighted area of the files to be transferred.

Single right-click
menu will change.
Point to the block labeled. **Send to**

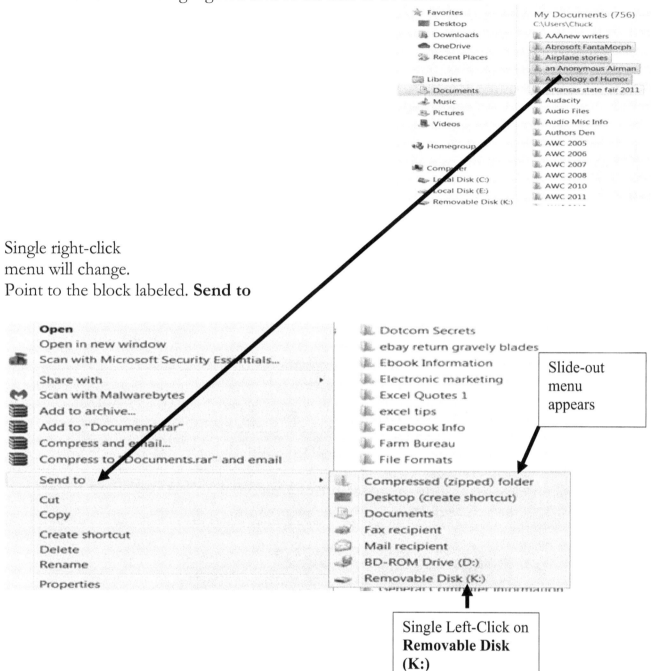

Files are copied to the external drive at this point

Capitalize or Uncapitalized a Word or Phrase

What: At times it is beneficial to be able to capitalize or uncapitalized a character, word, heading, phrase, or a paragraph for some special need.

Why: Capitalization of a word or phrase emphasizes the importance of word.

How: There are different methods of capitalization, which are determined by the goal of the writing.

Using the keyboard:
The keyboard is divided into two sections:
Lowercase characters
Uppercase characters

On most keyboards there are keys that have two symbols on the same key
The lower symbol is the lowercase
(letters on the keyboard only display lowercase)
The upper symbol is for uppercase letters and characters
(it is necessary to deep press the shift key to print in uppercase)

The shift keys on most keyboards are in a standard location
frequently identified by an arrow pointing up ⬆

Depress either key <u>simultaneously</u> with the key identifying the character to be capitalized

The key above the shift key is the Caps Lock key
When this key is pressed all characters typed after that will be uppercase
The caps lock key must be depressed a second time to turn this feature off

Alternative Method One   Changing the **Case** of highlighted text

It is also possible to alternate the appearance of text from:

      Lowercase to uppercase

      Uppercase to lowercase

      All uppercase

To change the **Case** of a word, line, or paragraph

Highlight text

      Press and hold shift key down

            Each time the F3 key is depressed it will change text:

                  From Lowercase to Uppercase

                  From Uppercase to Lowercase

                  Capitalize Only the First Letter of Each Word in Selected Test

Alternative Method 2

Highlight text to be modified

               Single left-clicking this icon

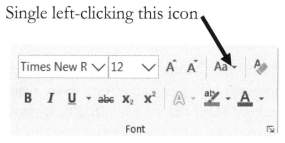

Drop-down menu appears

                      Sentence case.

                      lowercase

                      UPPERCASE

                      Capitalize Each Word

                      tOGGLE cASE

highlight option from menu to select appropriate change

Computer Memory

What: Stores information in various locations and formats.

Why: Information storage is a major function of a computer. It is used in order to store and allow the manipulation of data.

How: Without the ability to store and manipulate data, a computer would be little more than a typewriter. Information is stored basically in two types of memory.

RAM memory: Is a **R**andom **A**ccess **M**emory is a type of memory which is only active <u>while the computer has power</u>. When the computer is shut off, the data in RAM is lost. RAM resides on a chip inside of the computer. RAM memory allows the computer to work faster.

ROM memory: **R**ead **O**nly **M**emory is <u>residual memory and does not lose data when the power is off</u>. This type of memory resides in a Hard Disk Drive (HHD) and/or Solid-State Drive (SSD). It provides internal instructions to the computer on how to perform certain functions. In other words, it helps the computer understand what its capabilities are. Each time the computer is powered on, it searches through its ROM memory to determine what equipment is connected to it, and what computer programs are available for use.

Definitions:

Data is: Facts and statistics collected together for reference or analysis.

Information is: Raw or unorganized system (such as alphabets, numbers, or symbols)

Cloud Memory   Is a method of saving your files, but not on your computer. The data created is stored in another location. The advantages of such storage is that you can access your files wherever you have <u>internet access</u>. The disadvantage is your files are accessible by someone else (of course they're not supposed to look at your files). There is a possible charge for the service. A major advantage of this type of storage is that files can be readily shared.

Do not rely on cloud storage completely. Your files should be safe enough, but to be certain you can access your files, store them in your computer **and** on DVDs, flash drives, or another external medium.

Clearing Format

What: At certain times it is beneficial to remove all formatting of a document. Formatting does not affect the content of the text or illustrations of a document.

Why: When the formatting is removed from a document the attributes such as font, size, text (bold or italic), and color you applied in the text can be cleared and then <u>the text will return to its normal default style</u>. This allows a clean approach to reformatting the document.

How: <u>Before performing this operation save the file under another name.</u>
The purpose of this is to have a backup in case something goes wrong.
Work with a copy

Highlight the portion of the document where the formatting is to be removed.

If the document requires clearing of all formatting:
press **control and A** simultaneously
(this will highlight the complete document)

On the **Home** tab of the menu bar   single left-click

Menu bar

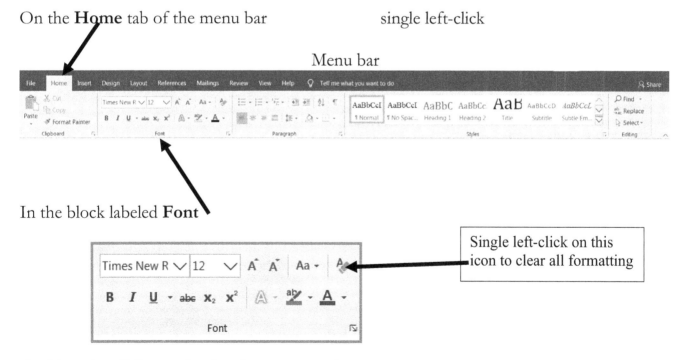

In the block labeled **Font**

Single left-click on this icon to clear all formatting

At this point all formatting has been removed

Creating a Header

What: Headers is the top section of the document and separates it from the main document. This information is repeated at the top of each page of the document.

Why: Headers provide a method of locating and identifying documents quickly

How: On the menu bar

choose the **Insert** tab   single left-click

Menu will change

In the block labeled **Header & Footer**   choose **Header**

single left-click

Menu will change

Choose appropriate block
By pointing and single left-click

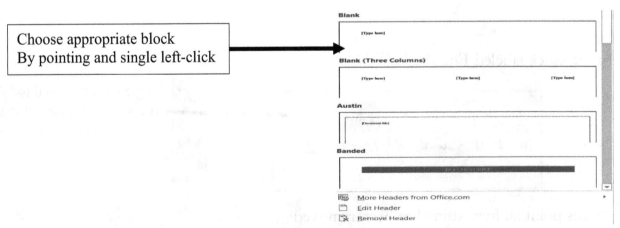

menu will change

[Type here]

Type in header information
    When information has been inserted
        Double left-click in the body of the document outside the header to
        close header

Creating a Footer

What: A Footer is the bottom section of a document, in a separate section from the main document. This information is repeated on bottom of each page of the document.

Why: Footers provide a method of locating and identifying documents quickly

How: On the menu bar

choose the **Insert** tab   single left-click

Menu will change

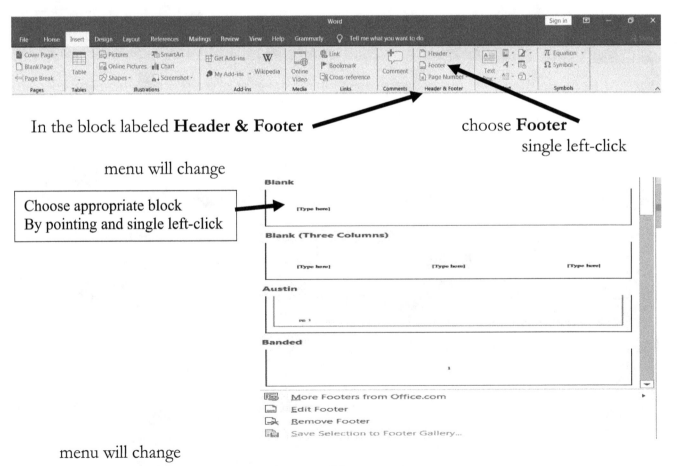

In the block labeled **Header & Footer**   choose **Footer**
                                                  single left-click

menu will change

Choose appropriate block
By pointing and single left-click

menu will change

[Type here]

Type in footer information
When information has been inserted Double left-click in the body of the document outside the footer to close footer

Creating a Table of Contents

What: A Table of Contents serves two purposes: It provides an overview of the document's contents and organization. It allows readers to go directly to a specific section of the document.

Why: A table of contents is important to the reader because it easy for the reader to locate different parts of the document.

How: The process of installing a table of contents is involved. There are three major steps.

        Step One   Copying the document and removing formatting.
        Step Two   Determining how the table of contents will be structured.
        Step Three   Determining where table of contents will be located.

Step One

Choose the document where the table of contents is to be inserted

The document must be copied in its entirety and saved with a different name. This will safeguard your data in case of a problem.
(See Snippets: Saving a file with another file name)
When copied, place cursor at the beginning of the new document single left-click

press Control A   this will highlight the complete document

Next, formatting must be removed for the complete document

on the **Home** tab

point at and single left-click

formatting will be removed from a document

click <u>outside of document</u> to remove highlighting

<u>You will now be working with a copy of your original document</u>

Step Two

It is now necessary to determine how the table of contents will be structured.

Return to the beginning of your document

on the **Home** tab

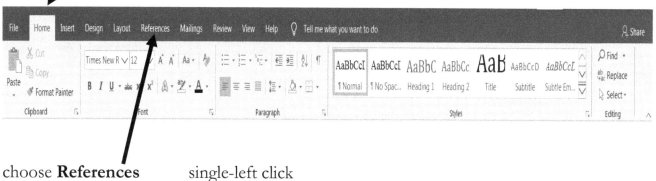

choose **References**   single-left click

menu will change

Single left-click on

menu will change

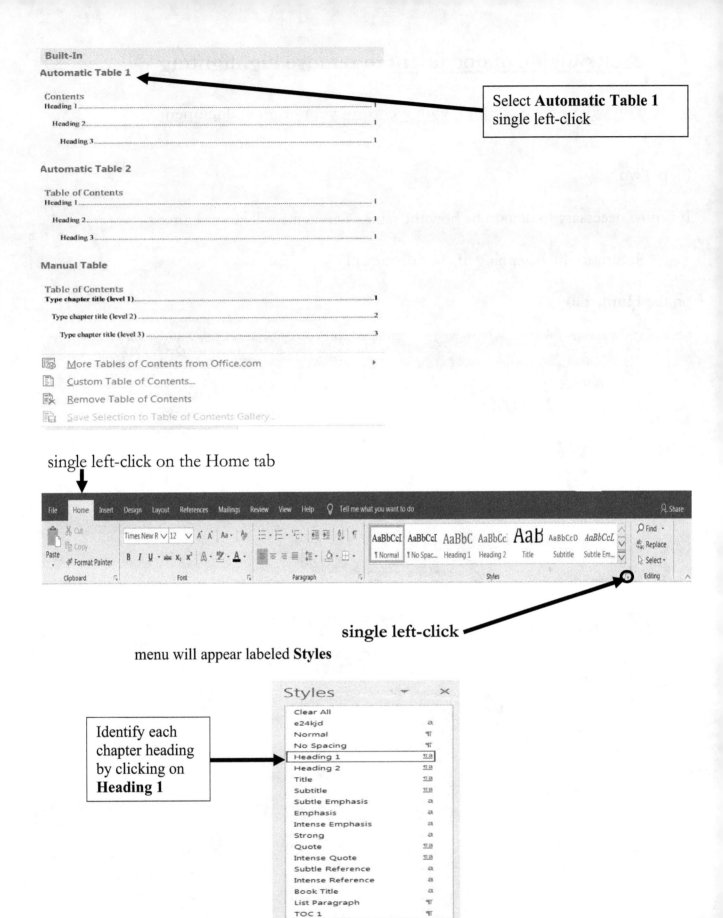

Built-In

Automatic Table 1

Contents
Heading 1 1
    Heading 2 1
        Heading 3 1

Automatic Table 2

Table of Contents
Heading 1 1
    Heading 2 1
        Heading 3 1

Manual Table

Table of Contents
Type chapter title (level 1) 1
    Type chapter title (level 2) 2
        Type chapter title (level 3) 3

More Tables of Contents from Office.com   ▶

Custom Table of Contents...

Remove Table of Contents

Save Selection to Table of Contents Gallery...

Select **Automatic Table 1** single left-click

single left-click on the Home tab

single left-click

menu will appear labeled **Styles**

Identify each chapter heading by clicking on **Heading 1**

54

click on References **tab**

Single left-click on Table of Contents again

menu will change

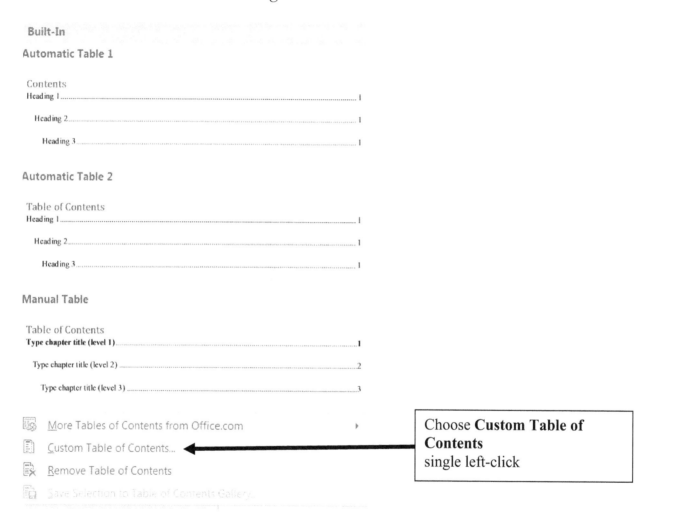

Choose **Custom Table of Contents**
single left-click

Menu will change

In the blocks for:
    Show page numbers
    Right aligned page numbers

If this book will be an <u>electronic book</u> which can be viewed on various devices, these two blocks should be **Unchecked**.

If this table of contents is being made for a document which will be printed on paper, **Do Not** remove the checks

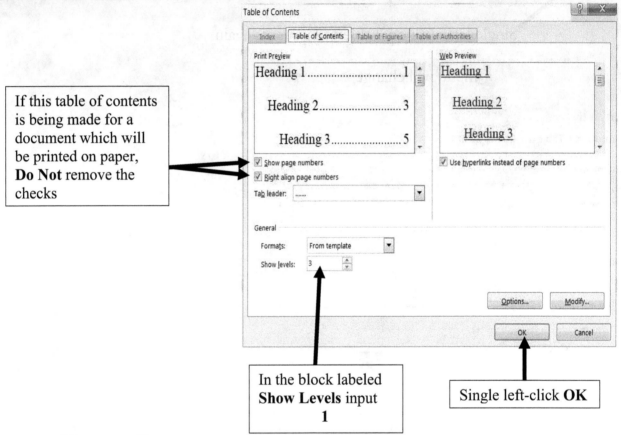

In the block labeled **Show Levels** input **1**

Single left-click **OK**

Message will appear

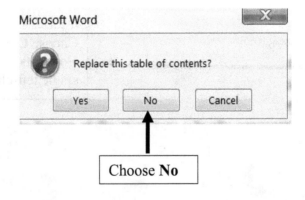

Choose **No**

Message will appear

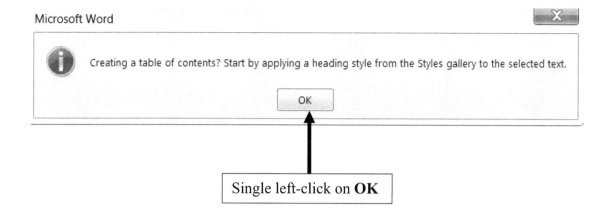

Single left-click on **OK**

Step Three

Determine where **Table on Contents** will be located. Single left-click on that location.

Choose **References** tab on the **Home** menu bar

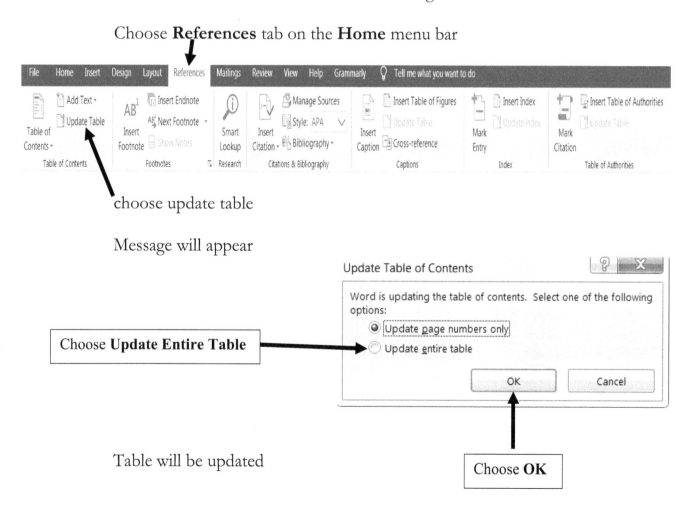

choose update table

Message will appear

Choose **Update Entire Table**

Choose **OK**

Table will be updated

If Table of Contents needs to be resized
Highlight entire table (which has just been created)

on the **Home** tab of the menu bar

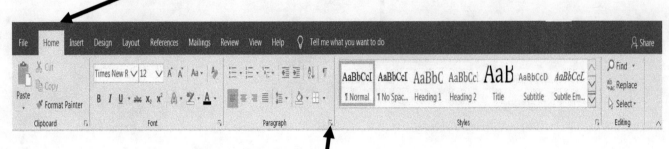

single left-click on down arrow in section labeled **Paragraph**

menu will change

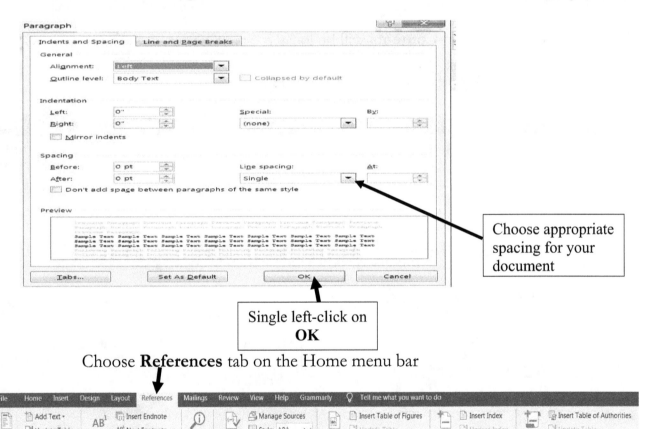

Choose appropriate spacing for your document

Single left-click on **OK**

Choose **References** tab on the Home menu bar

choose update table

Message will appear

Choose **Update page numbers only**

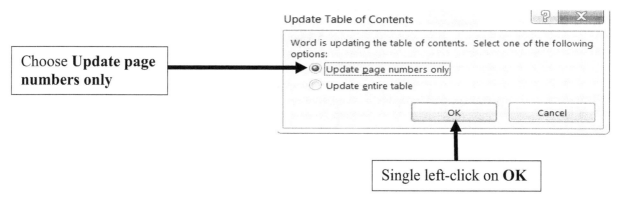

Single left-click on **OK**

Table of contents will now be in the appropriate location and updated

Remember you have been working with a copy.

Document should be renamed and saved as your completed document, it will also now be necessary to reformat the document (reestablish correct font, tabs, etc.) This is an excellent opportunity for a review of your document.

Note: A Table of Contents is easier to read if it is on a single page
                    If this is not possible, have them on facing pages (not back-to-back)

Creating an Index

What: An index is an alphabetical list of topics with reference to location.

Why: An alphabetical list of subjects with their location saves time and adds a professional touch to your work

How: There are three steps necessary for this process
1) Identify location of index
2) Identify topics for inclusion in index
3) Create index

Move to the end of the document to identify location of index
input the word **Index**

At this time, it is necessary to identify topics for the index
Return to the beginning of the document

On the **Home** tab   single left-click on **References**

menu will change

Single left-click on **Mark Entry**

menu will change

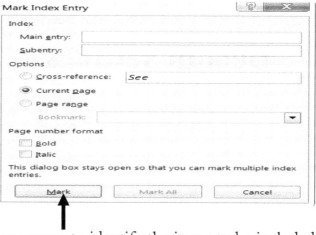

At this point it is necessary to identify the items to be included in the index
to do this highlight each topic for the index
single left-click on Mark
continue highlighting and clicking until all topics are identified

Move to the end of the document and place cursor below the word Index single left-click
return to **References** tab

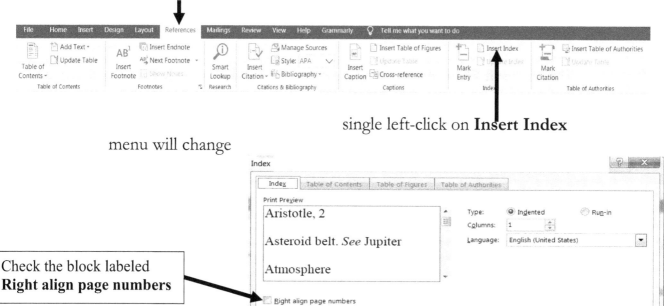

single left-click on **Insert Index**

menu will change

Check the block labeled
Right align page numbers

In the block labeled Formats
choose **From template**

Single left-click

The index will appear in the previously identified area, under **Index**

Note: an index is easier to read if it is on a single page
If this is not possible, have them on facing pages (not back-to-back)

Default Settings

What: Are preinstalled instructions, which tell the computer how to present information to the user. These settings can be adjusted by the user. They are also called presets or factory presets.

Why: Computer programs are not only powerful they are also versatile. If the settings could not be changed, the program would lose its versatility. Default settings determine how the information you input will be used.

The formatting of a document determines how it looks. It is possible to change not only the **Margins** on your document but also the type of **Font, Font Size** and the **Line Spacing**. By modifying these settings, time is saved and the document is presented in a professional manner.

How: The Microsoft Word program is an extremely powerful tool and it has many functions which make writing much easier.

For a writer, there are some changes that can be made which are beneficial.
You will begin by changing the default settings for the alphabet (**Font**). This is done by looking at the menu bar first.

Setting the Font
This is the menu bar for **Home**

In the block labeled **Font,**

Point at the arrow in the lower right-hand corner and single left-click

The menu will change to the **Font** menu

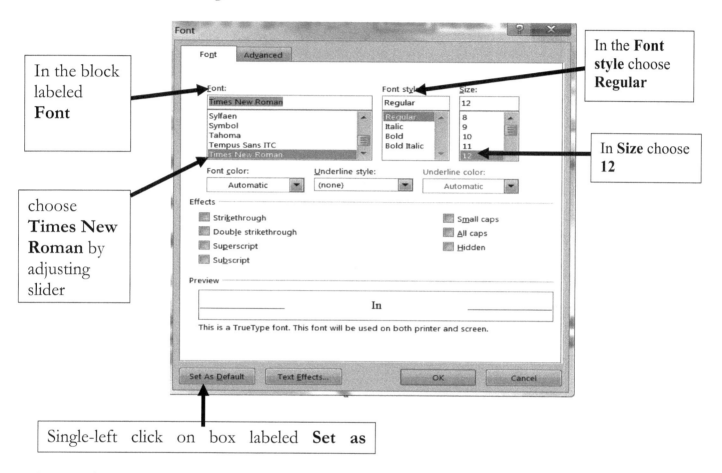

In the block labeled **Font**

choose **Times New Roman** by adjusting slider

In the **Font style** choose **Regular**

In **Size** choose **12**

Single-left click on box labeled **Set as**

Now, each time you access Word, you will be using this font for your documents. Times New Roman 12 is one of the most generally accepted fonts for writers

Setting Line Spacing and Indentation

Another important area of consideration is the **Paragraph** section on the menu bar.

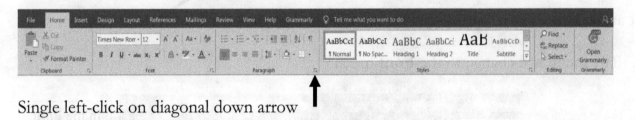

Single left-click on diagonal down arrow

A new menu will appear labeled **Paragraph**

in the area labeled **Indentation**

Change **Left** setting to **.5**

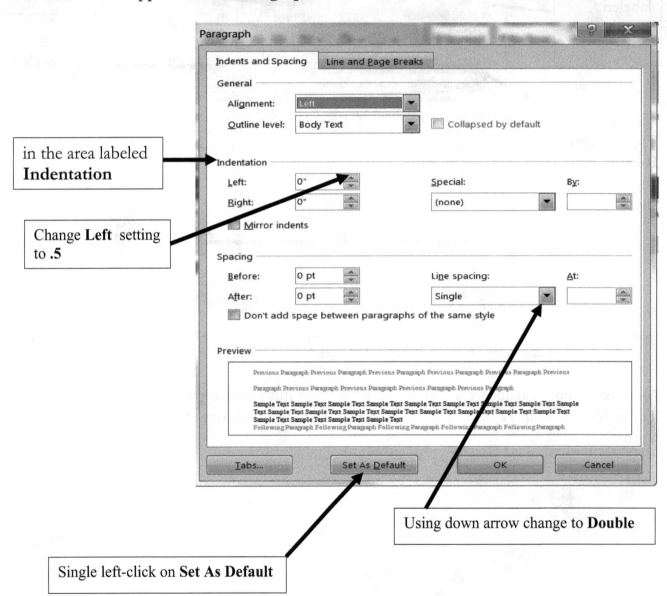

Using down arrow change to **Double**

Single left-click on **Set As Default**

Now, each time you open a new document in **Word**, it will be set up in this format. This is referred to as **Standard Document Format**

Encrypting Files

What: Encrypting files is a method of blocking access to sensitive information.

Why: Encryption is an important means to secure and protect sensitive data that you don't want anyone else to have access.

How: On the **Home** tab of the menu bar

choose the **File** tab   single-left click

The menu will change

Choose **Info**

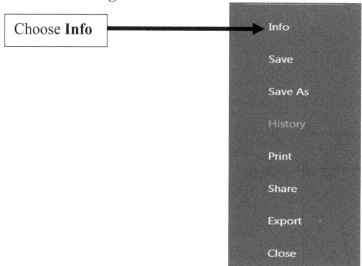

menu will change

Choose **Protect Document**

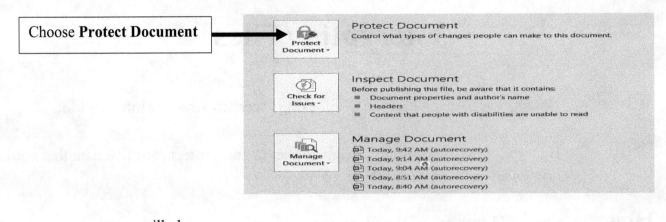

menu will change

Choose **Encrypt with Password**

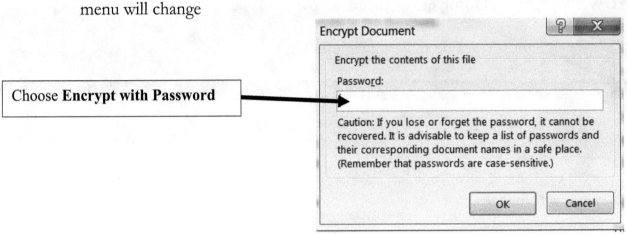

menu will change

Reenter password

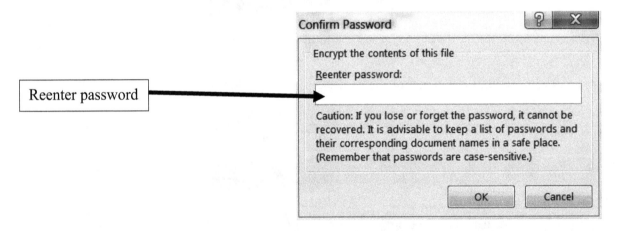

<u>**Document is now protected and can only be opened with Password**</u>

To undo protection:

Open document   (using password)

Copy document

Open new blank document

Paste document into new document

rename document

Files and Folders

What: The purpose of a file or folder is to store information.

Why: Information that you cannot located in is useless.

How: Computers store information in different locations so that it can be quickly located.
Your document when stored becomes a **File**
Similar files are saved in **Folders**
Folders are located in **Libraries**
Libraries are stored in ROM drives   (usually the C drive)

Computers store information in libraries. The information is organized according to content. The major categories are:
Documents.
Music.
Pictures
Videos

The writer is usually concerned with the **Documents Library**

The Process of Saving a File

Your document when saved becomes a **File**

It is stored in a **Folder**

Which is stored in the **Documents Library**

Which is located in an area referred to as:
All Libraries

It is wise to include the location of your document at the top of this page when saving it, with the date   (See Snippets   Creating a Header)

Example: lib.doc. my story. Chapter 1   01.01.XXXX

If you follow this procedure will be easy to locate the document of the later time

Finding a Word in a Document

What: Locating a specific word in a document is not difficult.

Why: On occasion is necessary to locate a word to verify spelling or modify it.

How: Open the document to be searched

On the keyboard press Control and F simultaneously

Menu will change

Input search word

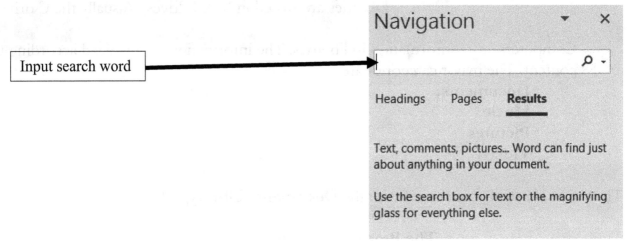

Word will automatically be highlighted in document

Menu will change

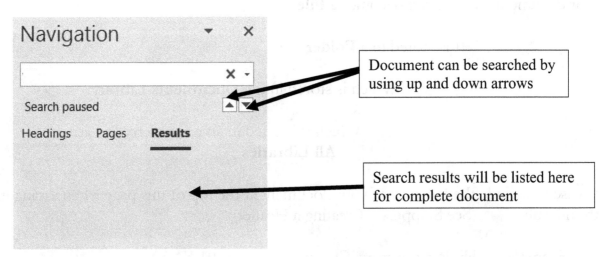

Document can be searched by using up and down arrows

Search results will be listed here for complete document

Modify document as needed

Finding a Word and Replacing it in a Document

What: Finding a word and replacing it in a document is not difficult

Why: On occasion is necessary to locate a word to verify spelling or modify it.
                   Example: Mary   and   merry

How: Open the document to be searched

          On the keyboard   press Control and F simultaneously

          Menu will change

Input search word

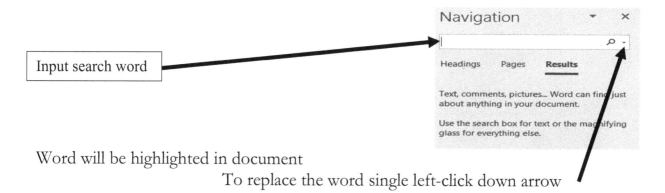

Word will be highlighted in document
                   To replace the word single left-click down arrow

               menu will change

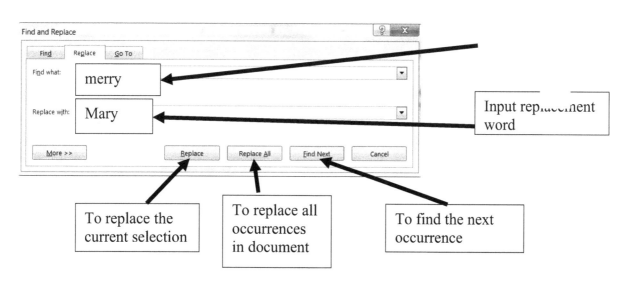

To replace the current selection

To replace all occurrences in document

To find the next occurrence

Finding Synonyms

What: A synonym is a word or phrase that means exactly or nearly the same as another word or phrase in the same language.

Why: Synonyms can help you express your ideas more clearly

How: Highlight a word in your document
>   Example: Now is the time for all good men

Single right-click on highlighted word

menu will appear

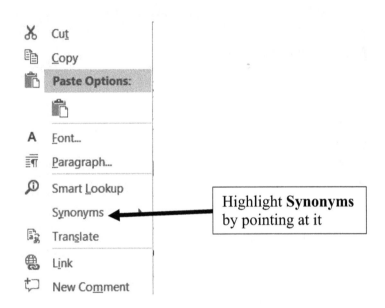

Highlight **Synonyms** by pointing at it

A slide out menu will appear

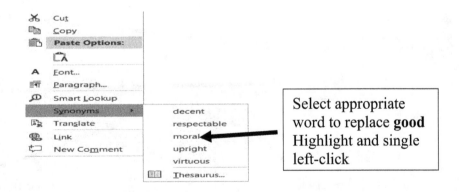

Select appropriate word to replace **good** Highlight and single left-click

The word **moral** will now have replaced the word **good**

Finding a Specific Page in a Document

What: Finding a page in a document is not difficult

Why: On occasion is necessary to go directly to a page in a large document.

How: Open the document to be searched

      On the keyboard   press Control and G simultaneously

      menu will change

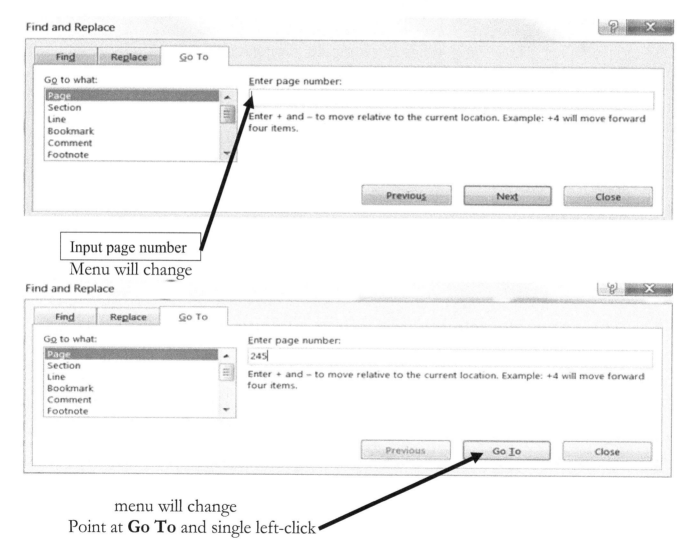

Input page number

Menu will change

menu will change

Point at **Go To** and single left-click

Page selected will appear on monitor

Highlighting

What: Text is highlighted in order to manipulate it.
Example: This is an example of highlighting *a word.*

Why: This is a time saving feature, which also enhances the capabilities of Word. With this feature, it is possible to manipulate words, sentences, paragraphs, and chapters quickly.

How:

Here are three nominal ways to highlight text:

One)   By left clicking using a mouse or trackball.
Two)   By left-clicking and maintaining pressure as you scroll.
Three)   Using the computer keyboard.

Method One

To highlight **a word**, place the cursor over the word and double left-click.

To highlight **a line**, place the cursor at the <u>extreme</u> left of the line, and single left-click.

To highlight **a paragraph**, place the cursor in the paragraph, and triple left-click.

Method Two

To highlight **specific text**, place the cursor at the beginning of the text, single left-click and hold pressure on that key, as you scroll. Release pressure when appropriate text is highlighted.

Method Three

Arrow keys

Place your cursor at the beginning of the text to be highlighted. Single left-click

Press either Shift key, then press the appropriate arrow key to highlight desired text.

Manipulating Text

To delete a word	highlight word	press Delete
To delete a sentence	highlight sentence	press Delete
To delete a paragraph	highlight paragraph	press Delete

Cut and Paste

To **Copy** text   highlighted word, sentence, or paragraph   press Control C
*(this **copies** the text without disturbing it)*

To **Cut** text   highlighted word, sentence, or paragraph   press Control X
*(this **removes** the text from one location, so it can be placed in another location)*

To **Paste** text   identify insertion point and   press Control V
*(this will allow you **to place the text** which was copied or cut **into another location**)*

Changing Case

Changing a letter to a capital or from a capital. This is called changing Case.

To change the Case of a word, line, or paragraph

Highlight text
Press and hold Shift key
Each time the F3 key is depressed, it will change text:
    From lowercase to Uppercase
    from Uppercase to lowercase
    Capitalize Only The First Letter of Each Word In Selected Test

Emphasizing Selected Text

To **Bold** highlighted text	control and B
To *Italianize* highlighted text	control and I
to <u>Underline</u> highlighted text	control and U

Highlighting a Large Block of Text

There are two nominal methods

Open document

Option One) Press Control and A   This will select <u>complete document</u>

Option Two) Used when a large portion of text is to be highlighted
   a) Place the cursor at the beginning of the text and single left-click
   b) Move cursor to the end of text
   c) Press shift and single left-click simultaneously

Selected text will be highlighted.

For extremely large blocks of text
   (example: a specific 75 pages of text need to be highlighted, of a 300-page document)
   a) Place the cursor at the beginning of the text and single left-click
   b) Use the up/down slider (on the right side of the screen) to move to end text

Slider

   c) Press shift and single left-click simultaneously

   selected text will be highlighted

Sorting a List Alphabetically

What: Organizing information alphabetically is easily accomplished

Why: It saves time and adds a professional touch to your work

How: Identify files to be sorted by highlighting

On the **Home** tab of the menu bar

In the block label Paragraph

point and single left click

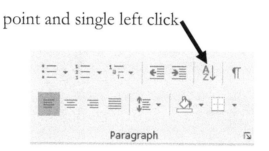

menu will change

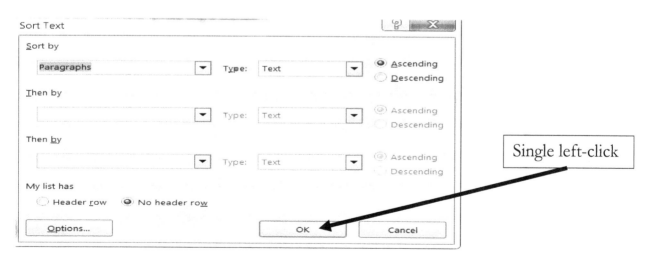

Single left-click

Files will be sorted alphabetically

Inserting Page Breaks

What: Place a page break in the document to start a new page

Why: This is useful when organizing a document

How: Single left-click in document where page break is to be inserted

On the **Home** tab of the menu bar   single left-click on **Layout** tab

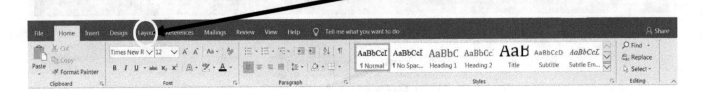

menu will change

In the section labeled **Page Set up**

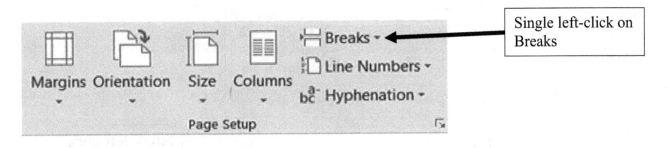

Single left-click on Breaks

menu will change

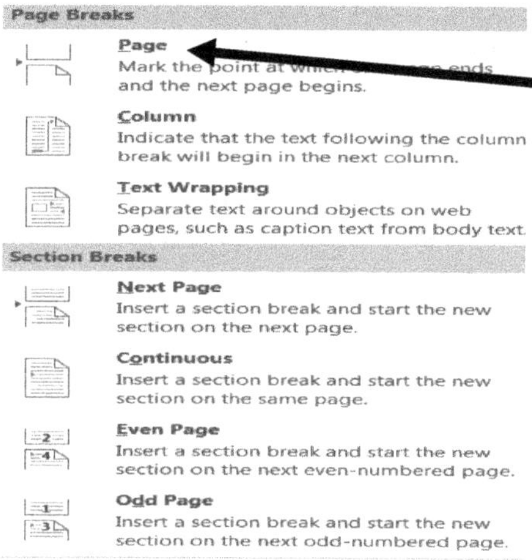

Page Breaks

Page
Mark the point at which ~~~~~ge ends and the next page begins.

Column
Indicate that the text following the column break will begin in the next column.

Text Wrapping
Separate text around objects on web pages, such as caption text from body text.

Section Breaks

Next Page
Insert a section break and start the new section on the next page.

Continuous
Insert a section break and start the new section on the same page.

Even Page
Insert a section break and start the new section on the next even-numbered page.

Odd Page
Insert a section break and start the new section on the next odd-numbered page.

Choose break option and single left-click

Page break is added

Inserting a Pictures

What: It is possible to insert photographs or screenshots into a document

Why: There are times when a picture can help in the communication of ideas, when coupled with words.

How: Determine the location of picture to be inserted in document
                     Single left-click on location

On the **Home** tab of the menu bar

Single left-click on the **Insert** tab

The menu will change

In the block labeled **Illustrations**

Single left-click on   **Pictures**

The menu will change

Select the location where the picture you wish to insert is stored
single left-click

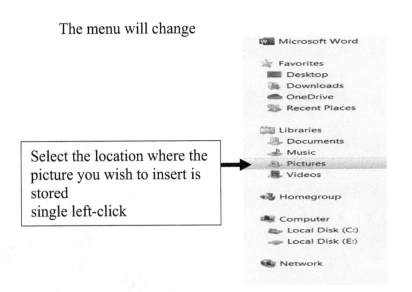

menu will change
highlight the picture to be inserted by single left-clicking on it
single left-click on block labeled **Insert**
Picture will be inserted

The size and location of this picture is adjustable by two different methods

Method One:

Left-click on <u>any</u> of the circles and holding the button down, scroll to adjust size

Method Two:

On the **Home** tab

of the menu bar in the block labeled **Paragraph**

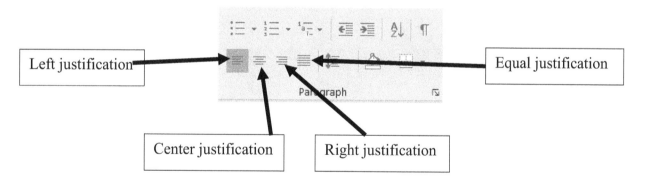

Left justification

Equal justification

Center justification

Right justification

Choose the location of your image by single left-click on indicated justification

The photograph is now inserted in your document
it can be fine-tuned adjusted by using controls on the keyboard
such as: space bar, back arrow, enter

Inserting a Shape

What: It is possible to insert numerous shapes into a document

Why: There are times when a shape, such as an arrow, circle, or block, can communicate more efficiently than words

How: Determine the location of the shape to be inserted in document
             Single left-click on location

On the **Home** tab of the menu bar

Single left-click on the **Insert** tab

menu will change

Single left-click on **Shapes**

menu will change

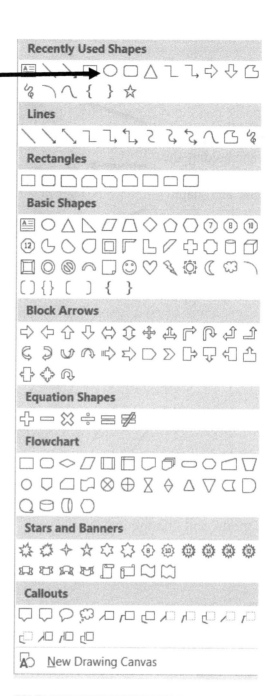

Nothing will happen until you move the cursor into the document

    This symbol will appear +

        move to the insertion point in document

            press left mouse button and   hold down

                insert shape by scrolling

                    when complete release left mouse button

shape is now in document

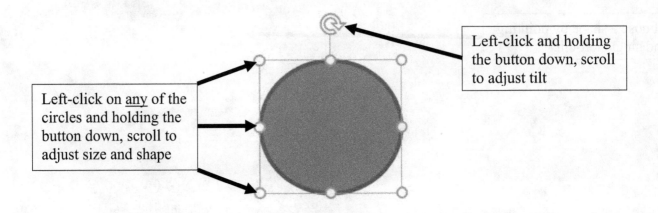

Left-click and holding the button down, scroll to adjust tilt

Left-click on <u>any</u> of the circles and holding the button down, scroll to adjust size and shape

Shape Styles menu appears

This menu provides you with options on how the shape will appear in the document

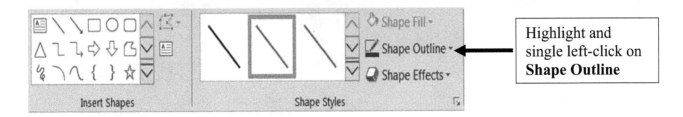

Highlight and single left-click on **Shape Outline**

menu will change

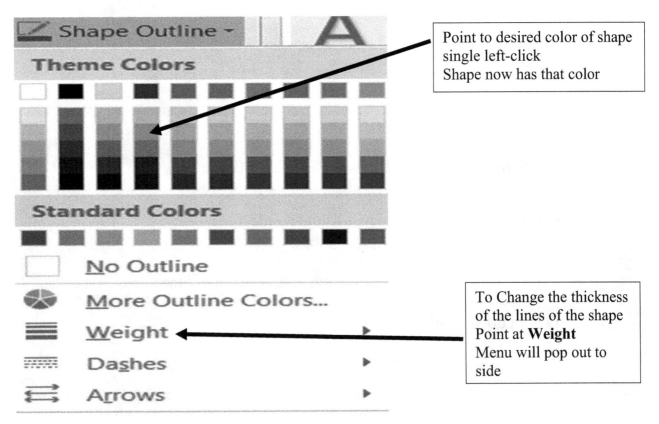

Point to desired color of shape
single left-click
Shape now has that color

To Change the thickness of the lines of the shape
Point at **Weight**
Menu will pop out to side

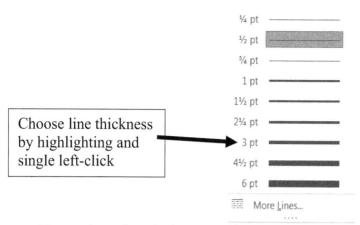

Choose line thickness by highlighting and single left-click

Example: the circle example selected above would now be displayed as

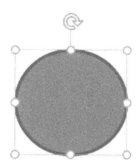

Remove the fill color   in this **Shape Styles** block

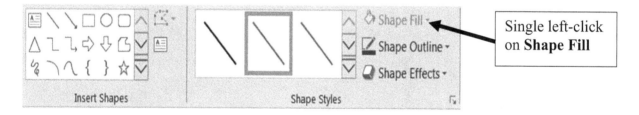

Single left-click on **Shape Fill**

Menu will change

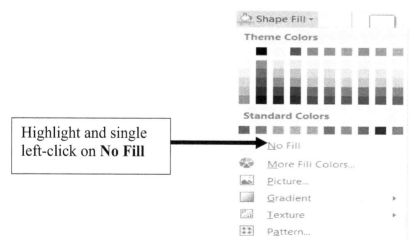

Highlight and single left-click on **No Fill**

The shape will now be displayed without fill	

If it is necessary to move the shape to a different location in the document
Place the cursor near the edge of the image

The symbol ⬌ will appear

Left click and hold the button down as you scroll and relocate image
Release button
when shape is in new location

Inserting Symbols

What: The addition of symbols to a document can be a valuable asset in clarifying your message. In most cases, it is possible to input them directly.

Why: Symbols add versatility and clarity to a document. It is possible to insert fractions (½), the degree symbol (°), pi (π), or currency symbols, such as the British pound symbol (£).

How:

Five Methods for Inputting Symbols

1) Direct input using keyboard
2) Using the alt key codes
3) Using the programs symbol tool
4) Using Windows Character Map
5) Change the Font family

Method 1   Direct Input Using Keyboard

Place your cursor in the document at the point where the symbol is to be placed.

Hint: For precise placement, Change the size of your font to a small number. Use the arrow keys on your keyboard to determine exact placement of the symbol. Then place symbol.

Example: input dollar sign
On the keyboard press shift and 4 simultaneously
The dollar symbol appears **$**

Method Two   Using the Alt Key Codes

Press the key on your keyboard labeled Alt and simultaneously press the numerical code for the symbol you wish to insert. (Refer to page 135 for a list of available symbols)

Special Note: This is only a partial list of the symbols. There are more than 100,000 available.

example: Alt 3 6   **$**   (this symbol will print)

Method 3   Use the Program Symbol Tool

Single left-click in your document where symbol is to be placed

On the **Home** tab of the menu bar
choose the **Insert** tab

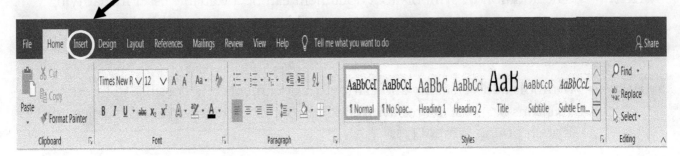

menu will change

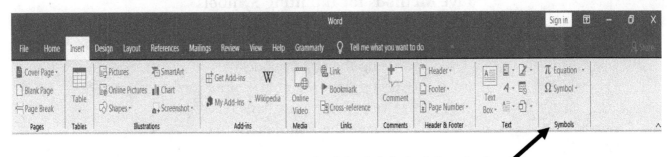

In the block labeled **Symbols**

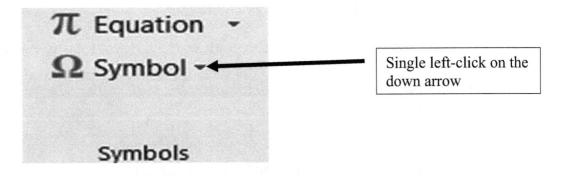

Single left-click on the down arrow

A drop-down menu will appear

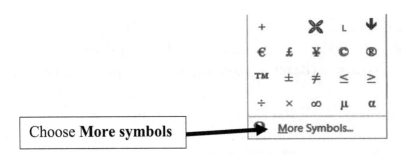

Choose **More symbols**

A drop-down menu will appear

Review available **Fonts** by clicking on down arrow

Review of available **Symbols** by clicking and dragging slider

Highlight symbol and single left-click

Single left-click on Insert

The symbol will be input

Method 4   Using Windows Character Map

This method is more complicated but it provides additional symbols

In the lower left-hand corner of desktop home screen

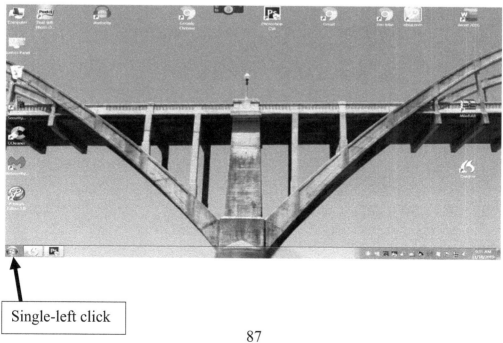

Single-left click

87

Pop-up menu will appear

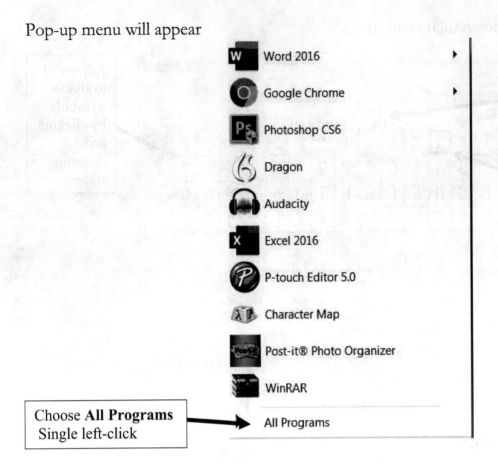

Choose **All Programs**
Single left-click

menu will change

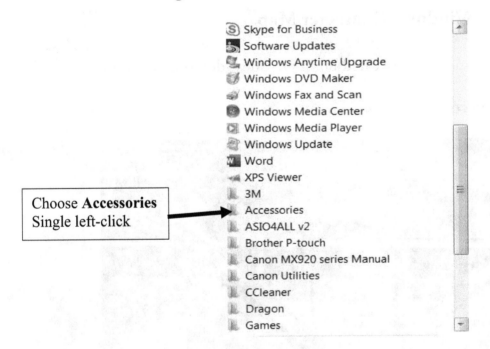

Choose **Accessories**
Single left-click

menu will change

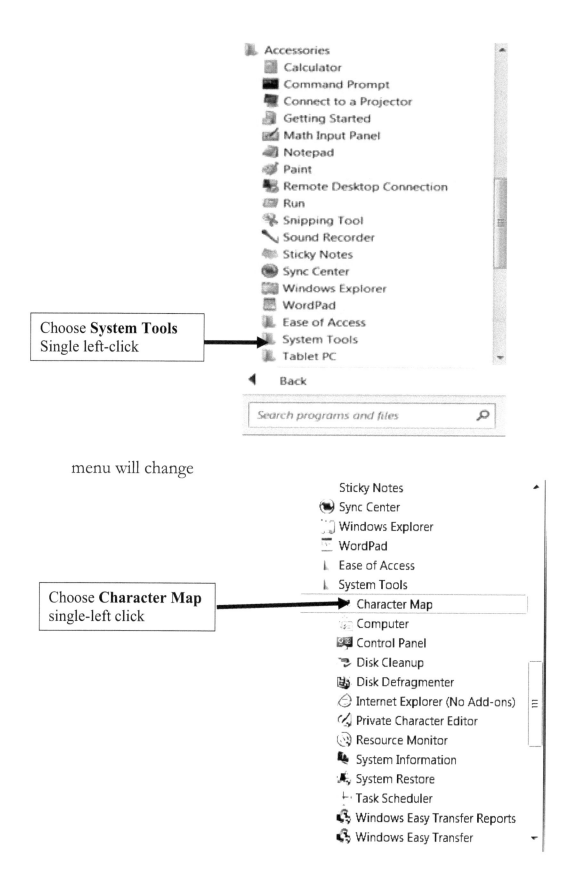

Choose **System Tools**
Single left-click

menu will change

Choose **Character Map**
single-left click

menu will change

89

It will be labeled **Character Map** and list available symbols

Special Note: *The top of the menu will be labeled for a font*
The listed symbols are for this font family…
Different font families have different symbols

example: Arial

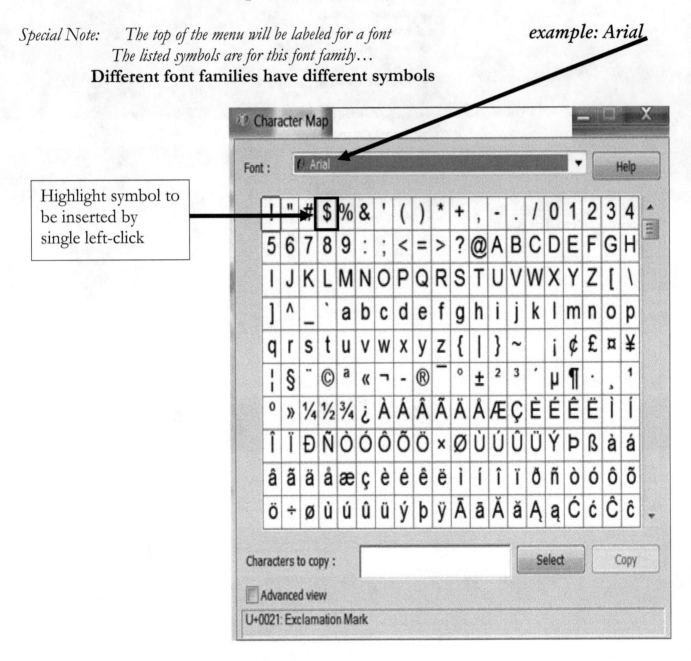

Highlight symbol to
be inserted by
single left-click

Then press control C (this will copy your selection)

Return to the document you wish to insert symbol in
Determine insertion point… Press control V
Symbol is inserted

Method 5   Change the Font family

There are many fonts which do not directly conform to an alphabet.

These fonts use symbols in place of conventional alphabet letters and numbers.

Examples include: (see section for **Alphabets Special Function Keys**)

Bookshelf Symbol 7	**Game Keys MT**	**Keyboard Keys**
PT Dingbats 1	**PT Dingbats 2**	**Shapes ST**
Webdings	**Wingdings**	**Wingdings 2**
Wingdings 3	(many others are available)	

To use the **Special Function Keys**
on the **Home** menu bar

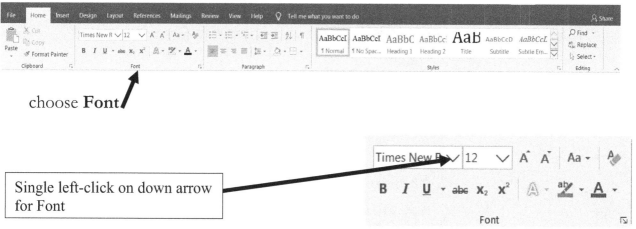

choose **Font**

Single left-click on down arrow for Font

Menu will change and list available Fonts

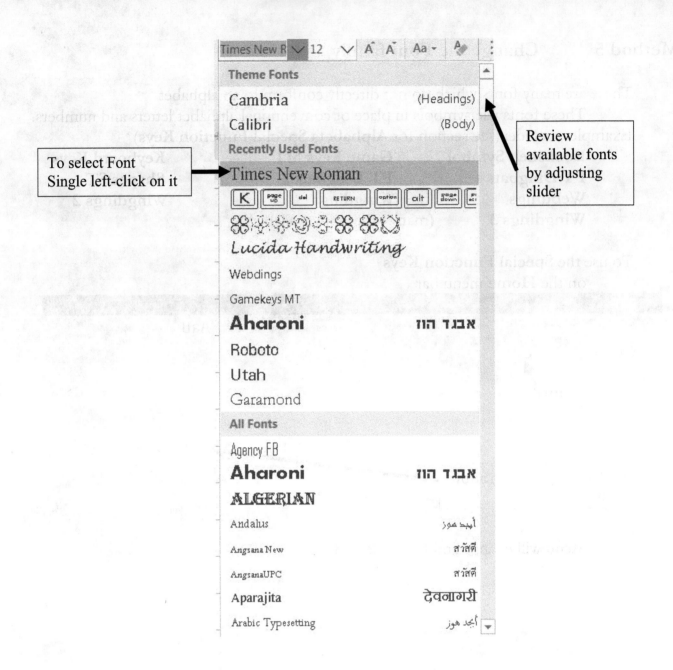

The font is now available for use in your document

Keyboard Shortcut Actions

What: Keyboard shortcuts are keys or combinations of keys, that provide an easier way to preformed functions which are usually done with the mouse.

Why: They typically invoke one or more commands using the keyboard that would otherwise be accessible only through a menu, or a pointing device. It is a much quicker way to accomplish work. Eventually, with use they will become a habit. Don't worry about memorizing all of them. Only use those you need.

How: Use the following keystroke combinations to perform the listed functions

Major Commands

Create new document	CONTROL + N
Opening existing document	CONTROL + O
Close active document	CONTROL + W
Save active document	CONTROL + S
Save as command	F12
Open print preview for active document	CONTROL + F2
Print active document	CONTROL + P
Open help menu	F1
Undo function	CONTROL + Z
Redo function	CONTROL + Y
Repeat last action	F4
Select next word to right	CONTROL + →
Select next word to left	CONTROL + ←
Select entire document	CONTROL + A

S

Copy selection to clipboard

Cut selection to clipboard

Paste selection from clipboard

Delete one character to left

Delete one character to right

Delete word to right

Display find what dialog box

Display go to dialog box

Start spellchecker

Display word count statistics

Remove all paragraph formatting

Create line break

Create page break

Move to start of line

Move to end of line

Move to start of document

Move to end of document

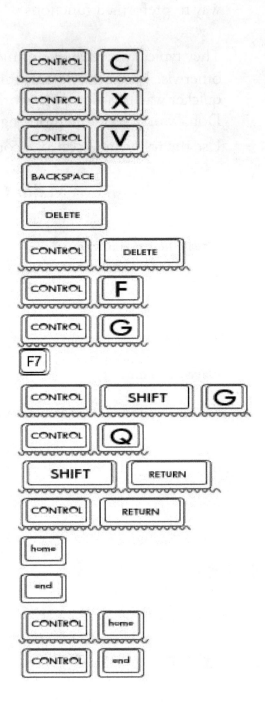

Line Numbering

What: Place a Line Number at the start of each line in a document

Why: This is useful when you need to refer to specific a line in a document, such as a script. It is extremely helpful when editing.

How: On the **Home** tab of the menu bar

single left-click on **Layout** tab

menu will change

In the section labeled **Page Set up**

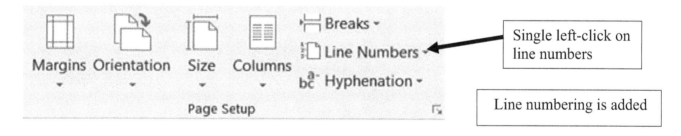

Single left-click on line numbers

Line numbering is added

Locating a Lost Document

What: Fugitive information is a fact of life when working with computers.

Why: For information to be valuable it must be accessible.

How: Locating misplaced information is not difficult

On the desktop screen of your computer

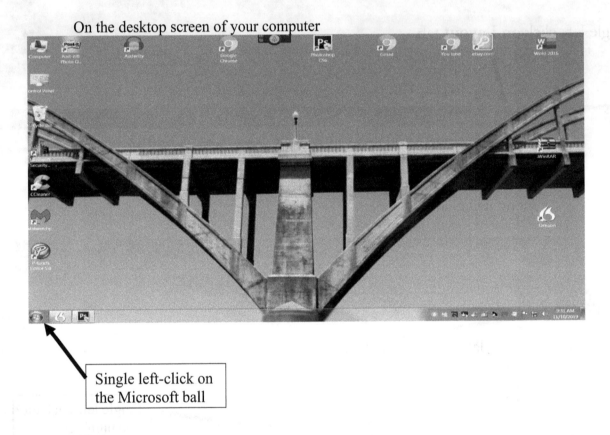

Single left-click on
the Microsoft ball

menu will change

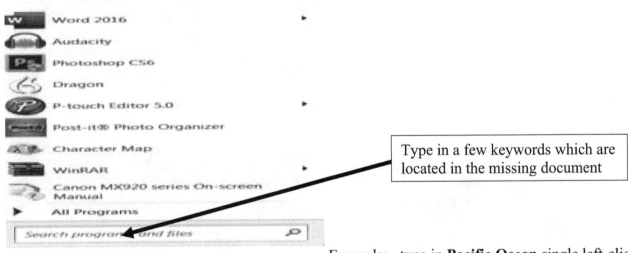

Type in a few keywords which are
located in the missing document

Example: type in **Pacific Ocean** single left-click

Microsoft Word will search your **Documents Library**

menu will change

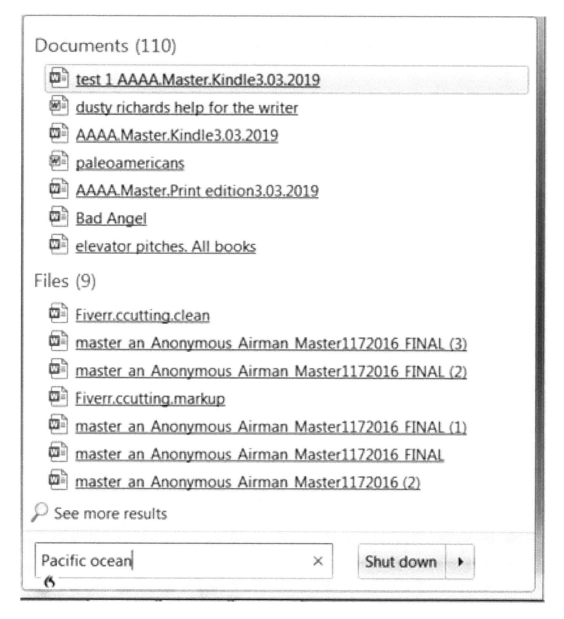

Highlight and single-left click on appropriate item

Document will appear on screen

Page Numbering

What: Page numbering is the process of applying a sequence to the pages to a document.

Why: Page numbers allow the rapid and systematic location of data and information.

How: Inserting page numbers is simple and there are many options for their location in a document.

On the **Home** menu bar menu bar

choose the tab labeled **Insert**

Single left-click

 The menu will change to the **Insert** menu

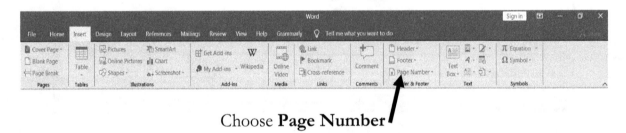

Choose **Page Number**

 menu will change

 At this point it is necessary to decide where the page number will be located in the document

For this example choose **Bottom of Page**

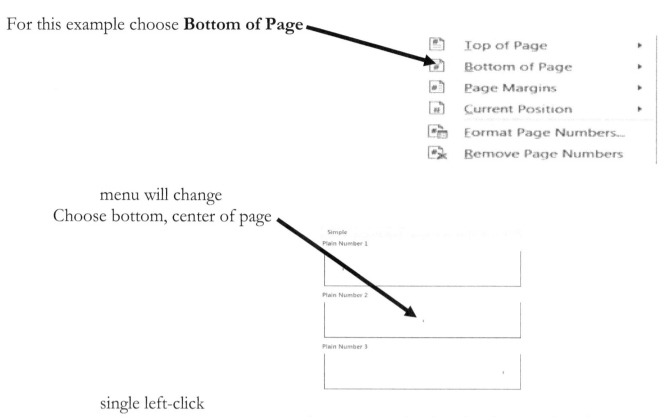

menu will change
Choose bottom, center of page

single left-click

page numbers are now in place for the complete document

Start page numbers on other than 1ˢᵗ page

This is a fairly complicated procedure, please read the instructions carefully

Summary: **There are four unique steps to this procedure**

Identify the location of the new first page
Split the document into two sections
Add numbers to the new section, starting at 1
Remove old numbers from original Section 1

In order to understand this process, the document formatting marks should be visible.
In order to do this:

On the **Home** tab of the menu bar

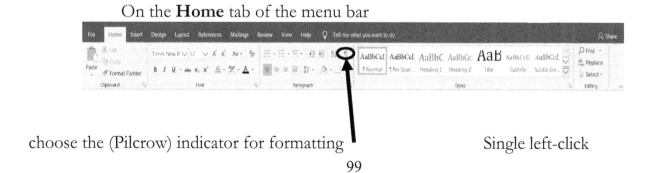

choose the (Pilcrow) indicator for formatting   Single left-click

Formatting marks will now be visible

Next determine the location of your new page 1 (it is necessary to begin breaking the document in half at this time.) This is done by placing the cursor in front of the first word of that page.

(In later steps, this section of your document will be referred to as document 2)

On the Home tab of the menu bar choose the tab labeled **Layout**   single left-click

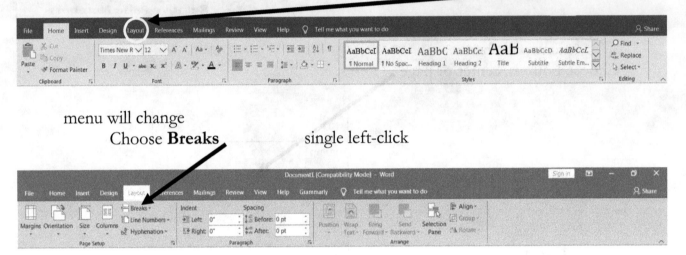

menu will change
   Choose **Breaks**   single left-click

Drop-down menu will appear labeled **Page Breaks**

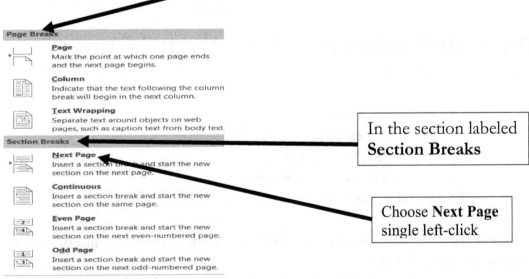

In the section labeled **Section Breaks**

Choose **Next Page**
single left-click

*At this point the document **has been** split into document 1 and document 2*
    (document 1 is the section of your document where you wish to remove page numbers)
    The next step is to unlink the two documents

Go to the top of the page (header) in the section of the document you want as page 1
    Double left-click
        graphic will appear

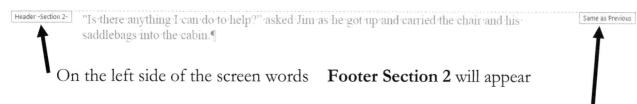

On the left side of the screen words **Footer Section 2** will appear

On the right side of the screen the words **Same As Previous**

<u>**This needs to be changed**</u>

place the cursor in front of the first word on the page you want to be page 1
single left-click

Menu will change to **Design**

choose **Link To Previous**

Message will appear

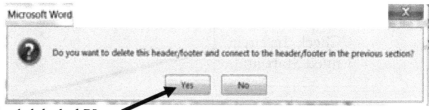

Single left-click on the block labeled **Yes**

As you click on this box, watch the section labeled **Same as Previous...** *it should disappear...if it doesn't*

Single left-click on **Link to Previous** *again*

on the Home tab of the menu bar
single left-click on the **Insert** tab

menu will change

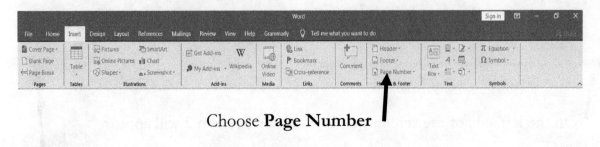

Choose **Page Number**

down menu will appear

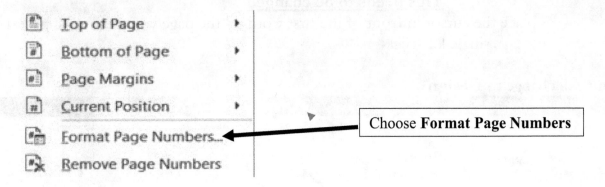

Choose **Format Page Numbers**

Menu will change

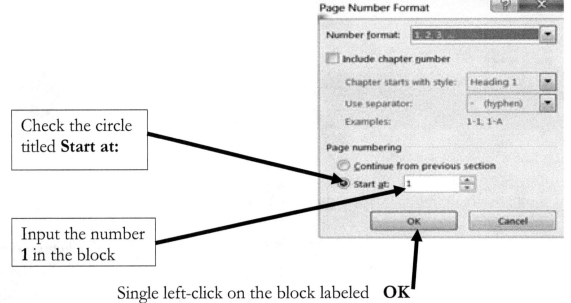

Check the circle titled **Start at:**

Input the number **1** in the block

Single left-click on the block labeled **OK**

At this point page numbers have been added to section 2
the next step is to delete the page numbers in section 1

Place your cursor on a page number **in Section 1**
      Identify **any** page number in this section and highlight it
          Press the delete key

The first pages in your document should be without numbers
      The first page in section 2 of your document should begin with a number 1
          Save the file

Creating a Quick Access Toolbar

What: The Quick Access Toolbar is composed of icons which allows rapid access to often used features. You determined what icons are listed in the toolbar.

Why: The use of this toolbar and will save you much time and effort in the future. It is quite simple to add or remove these and other icons.

How: On the Home tab of the menu bar

locate Quick Access Toolbar

This is an expanded section of the Menu Bar

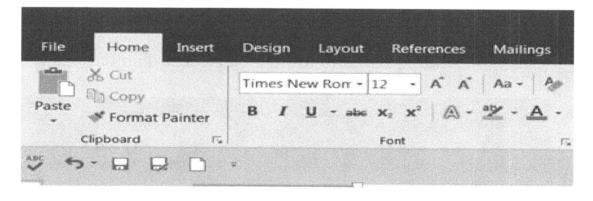

It is advisable to create a unique **Quick Access Toolbar,** which suits your needs. In the following example, 5 icons are used.

Example:(left to right) **Spellchecker**

> **Undo**
>
> **Save**
>
> **Save As**
>
> **New Document**

What do these icons do?

These features are activated by highlighting and single left-clicking

Spellchecker   Identifies and provides corrected spelling and grammar issues for an open document.

Undo   Deletes last item input. Each click on this icon reverses your last action. Extremely useful.

Save   Causes a copy of the current document or image to be saved.

Save-As   Automatically saves current document under <u>another filename</u>. You will be prompted for a new filename. Very helpful for organizing documents later retrieval.

New document   Creates a new blank document.

Adding Icons to the Quick Access Toolbar

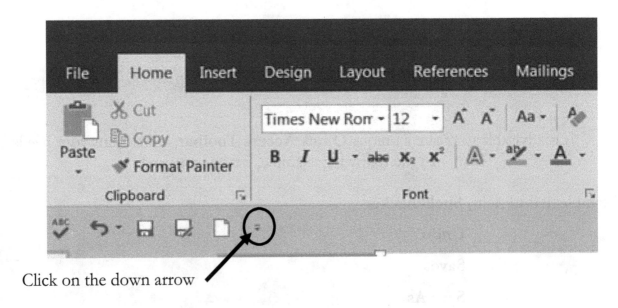

Click on the down arrow

menu will change

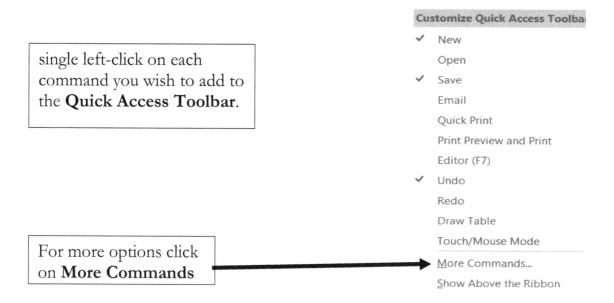

single left-click on each command you wish to add to the **Quick Access Toolbar**.

For more options click on **More Commands**

Menu will change to:

Word Options Menu

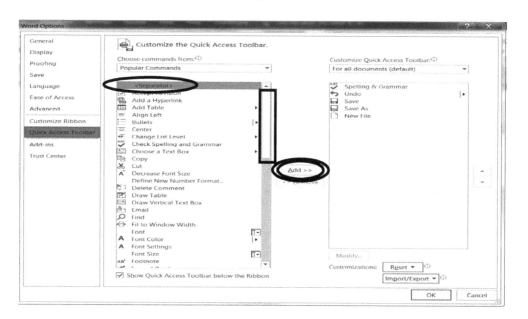

In the section labeled **Separators**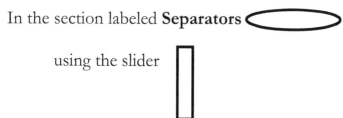

using the slider

scroll through the list and highlight the item to be added

To add this feature to the quick access toolbar, point and single left-click on the block

labeled **Add**

Be selective in what you choose… Try to keep it simple.

When you are finished click on the block labeled **OK**

The menu will disappear and you will be returned to your document.

To remove icons from the quick access toolbar,

highlight item and then use **Remove**

Each time you access **Word**, these features will be available.

Quote Marks

What: There are two different kinds of quotes marks

Why: The quote marks have two major different functions.
1)   To identify dialogue
2)   Used only when identifying feet and inches

How: **Type 1**   used only when **Identifying Dialogue**

    "   this is a double Smart Quote   (Open quote)
    "   this is a double Smart Quote   (Close quote)
    '   this is a single   Smart Quote   (apostrophe)

    Type 2   used only when **Identifying Feet and Inches**

    "   this is a double Straight Quote   (inches)
    '   this is a single Straight Quote   (feet)

Method to switch from smart quotes to straight quotes and vice versa

On the **Home** tab of the menu bar

single left-click on **File**

drop-down menu will appear

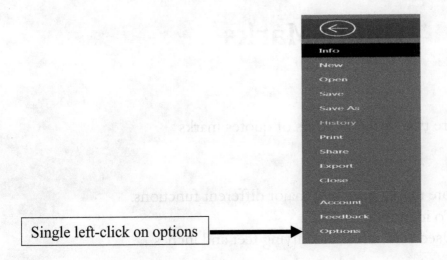

Single left-click on options

menu will appear

Word Options

Highlight and single left-click on **Proofing**

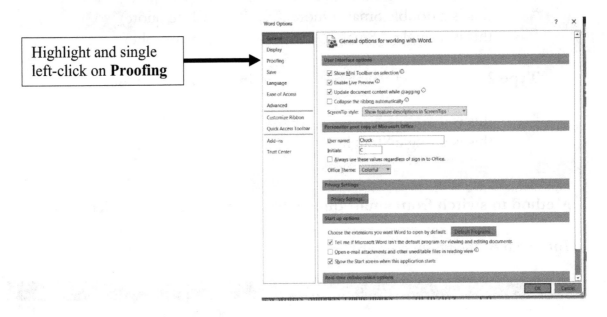

menu will change

Highlight and single left-click
on **AutoCorrect options**

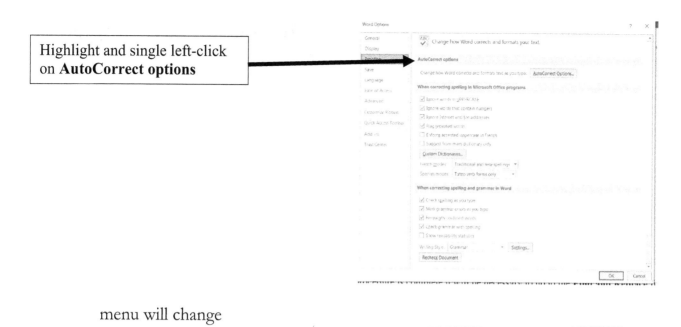

menu will change

Single left-click on
Autoformat As You Type

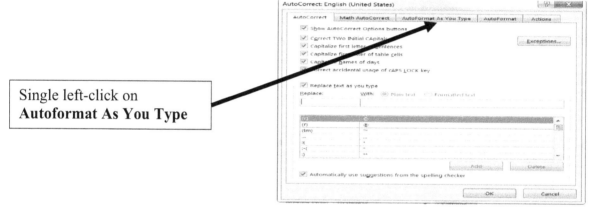

menu will change

Click on the box labeled
Straight quotes with
smart quotes

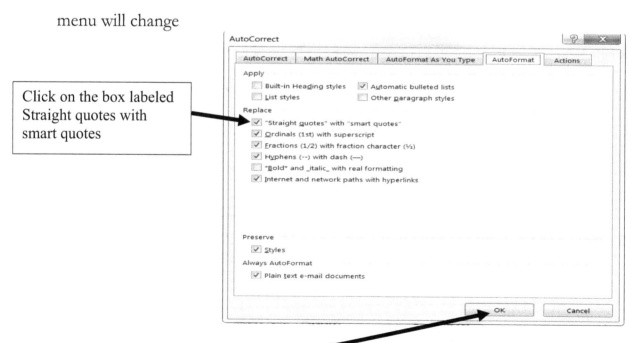

Single left-click on okay

If you are proofing a document which is already completed

After the above procedure is completed, it will be necessary to go to the **Find and Replace** function

Press Control F simultaneously this will open the Navigation menu

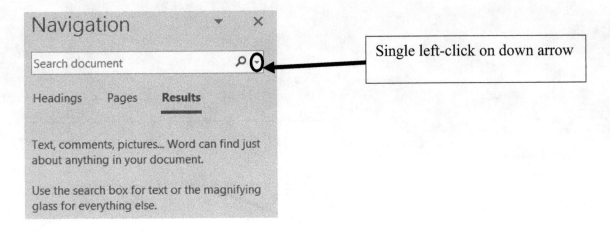

Single left-click on down arrow

menu will change

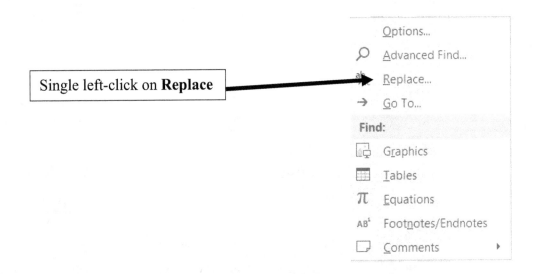

Single left-click on **Replace**

menu will change

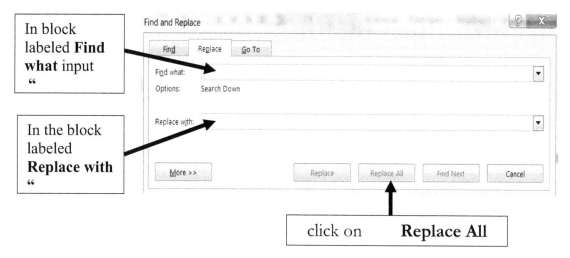

In block labeled **Find what** input
"

In the block labeled **Replace with**
"

click on **Replace All**

All quotes will be replaced in the format you previously selected

Reverse this procedure to switch back

Saving Files

What: One of the most important functions of the computer is its ability to save information. This is easily accomplished in a number of ways.

Why: Information is useless <u>if it cannot be located</u>.

How: There are different ways to save files in the computer

There are two major ways to save your work in Word:

Method 1   **Save**

Method 2   **Save As**

Additionally, there are different ways to do this:

Option A   Using **File** command on the menu bar.
Option B   Using the **Quick Access Toolbar.**

There are many options available to the writer for storing their work. In most instances, this will be accomplished by storing the document in one of the computer's libraries which is named **Documents**.

Your actual document will be a **<u>File</u>**, in this case named **My Story**

Additionally, files can be saved using the commands:

Save   This method saves the file under its <u>own file name</u>

Save As   This method saves the file under <u>another file name</u>

The **Save As** command is used to save a file in a <u>different location</u>. This is beneficial when more than one copy of the file is needed for different purposes.

Example: A short story has been entered in a contest, along with two other entries of yours. This story will be in a folder titled Contest Entries.

You also wish to save this file in another folder named Short Stories.

Although this may appear confusing, as your writing skills progress you will find it quite logical, simple and beneficial.

In most situations, you will only use the **Save Command**

Saving a File using the File Command.

(Method 1)

On the **Home** tab of the menu bar
single left-click on **File**

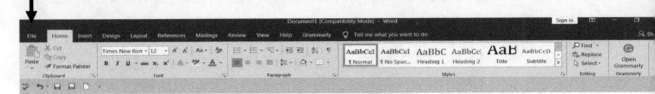

Screen will change and display the **File Menu**

Point and single left-click on **Save**

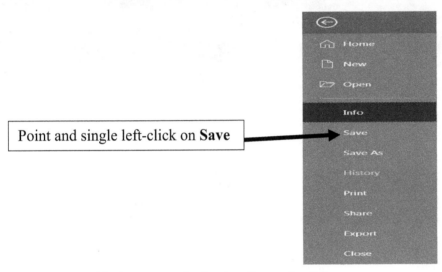

The screen will change and display **Save As Menu**

*Special Note: It may seem strange that the **Save-As** Menu will appear instead of the **Save** Menu.
This will occur only the first time a new document is saved.
Word must have a filename in order to store and locate the file.*

Point at **Browse** single left-click

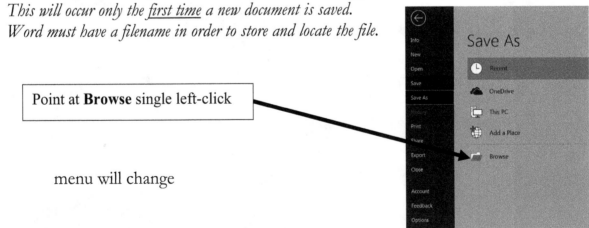

menu will change

In the block labeled **File name** input **My Story**

By default, the first few words of your document will be highlighted as the filename.

Highlighting will disappear as you type the new file name

Click on **Save**

Your work is now saved and it is located in the **Documents Library**

Saving a file using the Save As file command

On the **Home** tab of the menu bar
single left-click on **File**

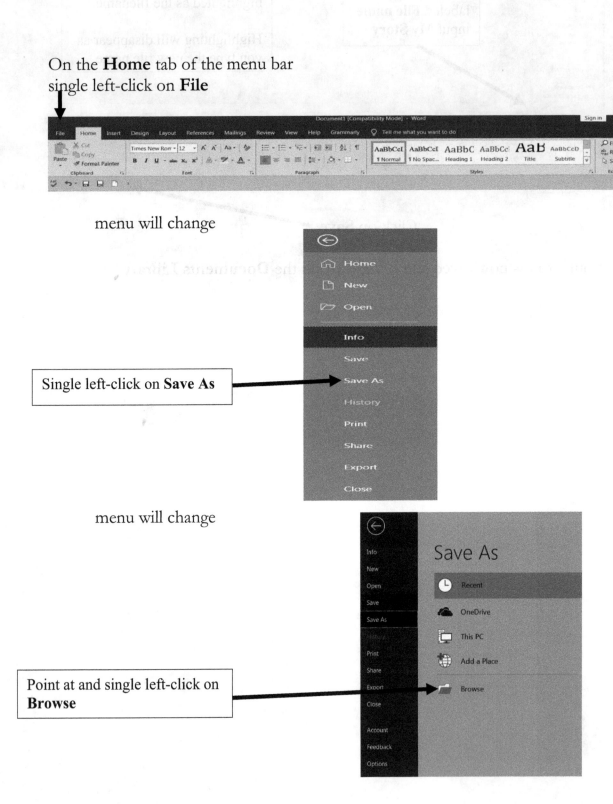

menu will change

Single left-click on **Save As**

menu will change

Point at and single left-click on
Browse

menu will change

In the block
labeled

In the block labeled **File name** input **My Story 2**

Click on **Save**

Your work is now saved and it is located in the **Documents Library** *with a new name*

Saving the File Using the Quick Access Menu

(Option 2)

This process is simpler and faster than **Option One**

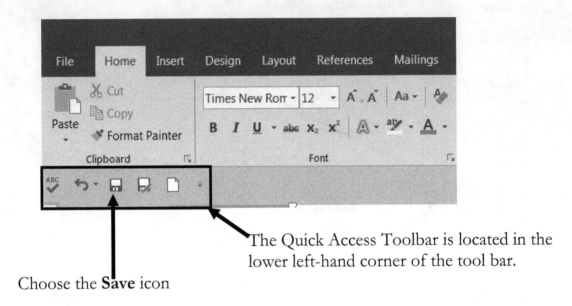

The Quick Access Toolbar is located in the lower left-hand corner of the tool bar.

Choose the **Save** icon

The screen will change and display **Save As Menu**

Special Note: It may seem strange that the **Save-As** *Menu will appear instead of the* **Save** *Menu.*
This will occur only the <u>first time</u> a new document is saved.
Word must have a filename in order to store and locate the file.

menu will appear:

Point at and single left-click
on **Browse**

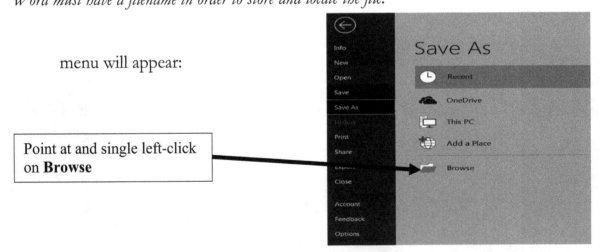

menu will change, and display the **Documents Library**

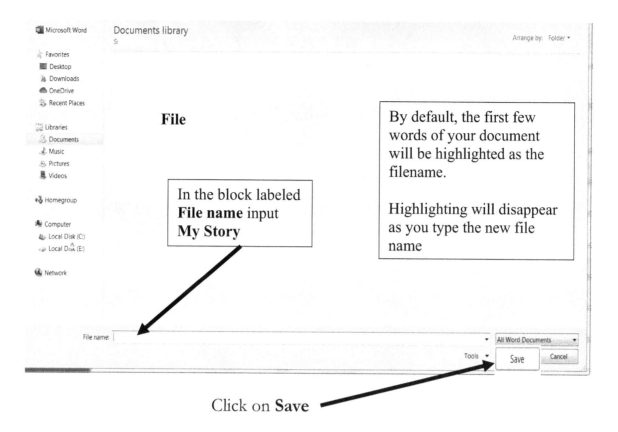

Click on **Save**

Your work is now saved and it is located in the **Documents Library**

Using the Save As Command on Quick Access Menu

Option One

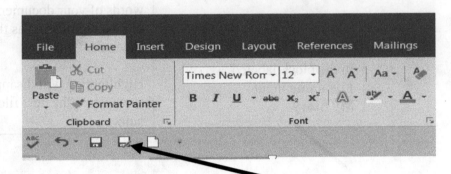

On the menu bar single left-click on the **Save As** icon
menu will change

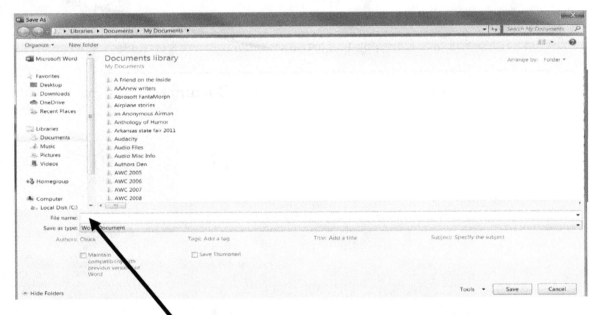

In the block labeled **File name** your current filename will automatically be inserted.

(It is possible to rename this file at this point by typing over highlighted folder or file name.)
If desired, input new filename. If the block is blank there is no problem.

Extremely Important Notice
If a filename already exists in the File name block, be extremely cautious.
If you input a new filename it will <u>replace</u> the file in that location.
This means any information stored on the original file will be rewritten.

In the lower right-hand corner, single left-click on **Save**
The file has now been saved at this location.

Option B   Create a new location for your file.

The menu will change,
and the block will appear highlighted in the Documents Library labeled.
>   New Folder

input the name of the new folder in that block.

Single left-click on the block labeled Open

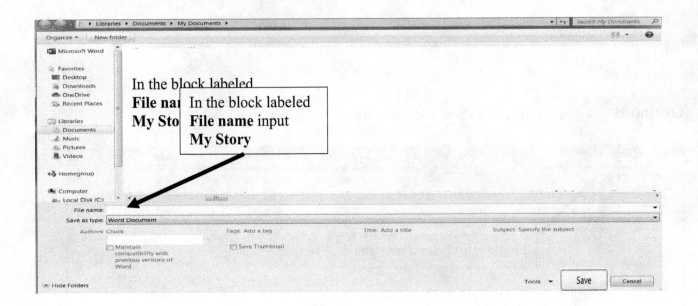

As you input the filename. The block that was labeled **Open**
changes to the word **Save**

single left-click on **Save**

Your work is now saved in the new folder you just created.

and your document –**My Story** –

it is located in that folder – in the **Documents Library**

As you complete each chapter in your book – they will be saved in the folder titled **My Story**

Example: **Documents Library**

My Story

Chapter 1 The Beginning

Chapter 2 The Middle

+   **Chapter 3 The Closure**

Alphabets

Special Function Keys

Bookshelf Symbol 7

To use these codes, it is necessary to input **Bookshelf Symbol 7** in the font block
On the Home tab of the menu bar

In the block labeled **Font**   single left-click on the down arrow

Drop down menu will appear
choose **Bookshelf Symbol 7**
by single left-click

Lower case

a	b	c	d	e	f	g	h	I	j	k	l	m	n
∾	∴	♩	⌢	‿	♮	°	⚘	✕	\$	∓	≐	≠	↘

o	p	q	r	s	t	u	v	w	x	y	z
↗	✓	⌐	‴	----	▪	✳✳	✳✳	♥	♠	⌢	‿

Upper Case

A	B	C	D	E	F	G	H	I	J	K	L	M	N
X́	ȳ	á	à	ã	í	ì	ᴜ	ú	ù	ʎ́	ʎ	ə́	ə̀

O	P	Q	R	S	T	U	V	W	X	Y	Z
ɔ́	ɔ̀	ɔ́	ɔ̀	ɔ̃	ɛ̃	æ	œ́	œ̃	ʤ	ŋ	ɪ́

Numbers lower case

1	2	3	4	5	6	7	8	9	0	-	=
Ḿ	m̨	Ǹ	Ṕ	ṕ	Ṕ	Q́	q́	Q̀	í	H́	T̄

Numbers upper case

1	2	3	4	5	6	7	8	9	0	-	=
ă	V̌	ƅ	B̌	C̀	⌄	Q́	q́	Q̀	í	H́	Ǵ

Game Keys MT

To use these codes, it is necessary to input **Game Keys MT** in the font block
On the Home tab of the menu bar

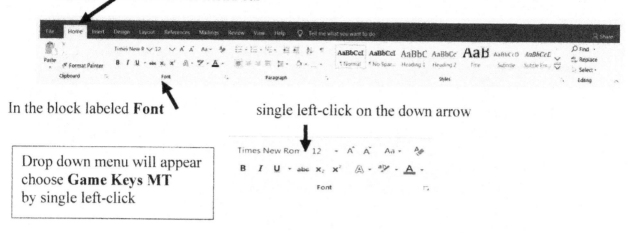

In the block labeled **Font**   single left-click on the down arrow

Drop down menu will appear
choose **Game Keys MT**
by single left-click

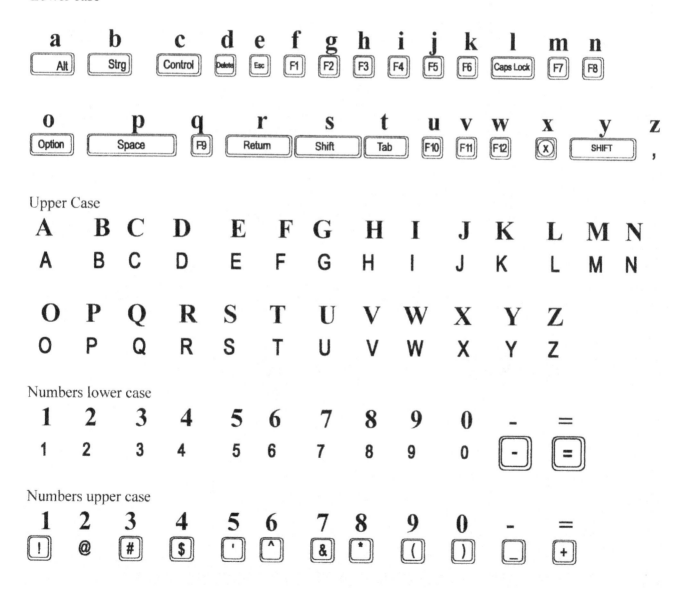

Lower case

a	b	c	d	e	f	g	h	i	j	k	l	m	n
Alt	Strg	Control	Delete	Esc	F1	F2	F3	F4	F5	F6	Caps Lock	F7	F8

o	p	q	r	s	t	u	v	w	x	y	z
Option	Space	F9	Return	Shift	Tab	F10	F11	F12	X	SHIFT	,

Upper Case

A	B	C	D	E	F	G	H	I	J	K	L	M	N
A	B	C	D	E	F	G	H	I	J	K	L	M	N

O	P	Q	R	S	T	U	V	W	X	Y	Z
O	P	Q	R	S	T	U	V	W	X	Y	Z

Numbers lower case

1	2	3	4	5	6	7	8	9	0	-	=
1	2	3	4	5	6	7	8	9	0	-	=

Numbers upper case

1	2	3	4	5	6	7	8	9	0	-	=
!	@	#	$	'	^	&	*	(	)	_	+

Keyboard Keys

To use these codes, it is necessary to input **Keyboard keys** in the font block
On the Home tab of the menu bar

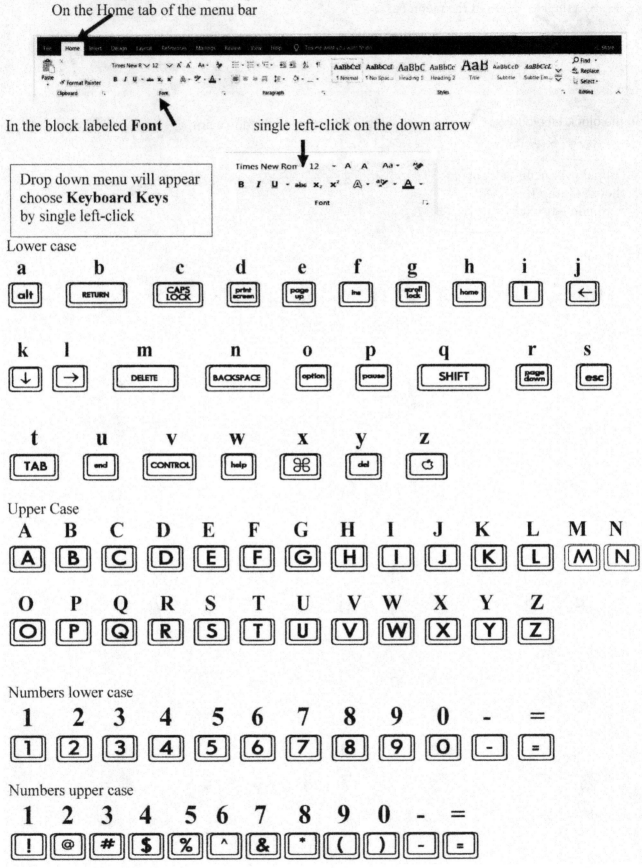

In the block labeled **Font**   single left-click on the down arrow

Drop down menu will appear
choose **Keyboard Keys**
by single left-click

Lower case

a — alt   b — RETURN   c — CAPS LOCK   d — print screen   e — page up   f — ins   g — scroll lock   h — home   i — | j — ←

k — ↓   l — →   m — DELETE   n — BACKSPACE   o — option   p — pause   q — SHIFT   r — page down   s — esc

t — TAB   u — end   v — CONTROL   w — help   x — ⌘   y — del   z —

Upper Case

A B C D E F G H I J K L M N

O P Q R S T U V W X Y Z

Numbers lower case

1 2 3 4 5 6 7 8 9 0 - =

Numbers upper case

1 2 3 4 5 6 7 8 9 0 - =

! @ # $ % ^ & * ( ) - =

126

PT Dingbats 1

To use these codes, it is necessary to input **PT Dingbats 1** in the font block
On the Home tab of the menu bar

In the block labeled **Font**

Drop down menu will appear
choose **PT Dingbats 1**
by single left-click

single left-click on the down arrow

Lower case

a   b   c   d   e   f   g   h   I   j   k   l   m   n

o   p   q   r   s   t   u   v   w   x   y   z

Upper Case

A   B   C   D   E   F   G   H   I   J   K   L   M   N

O   P   Q   R   S   T   U   V   W   X   Y   Z

Numbers lower case

1   2   3   4   5   6   7   8   9   0   -   =

Numbers upper case

1   2   3   4   5   6   7   8   9   0   -   =

PT Dingbats 2

To use these codes, it is necessary to input **PT Dingbats 2** in the font block
On the Home tab of the menu bar

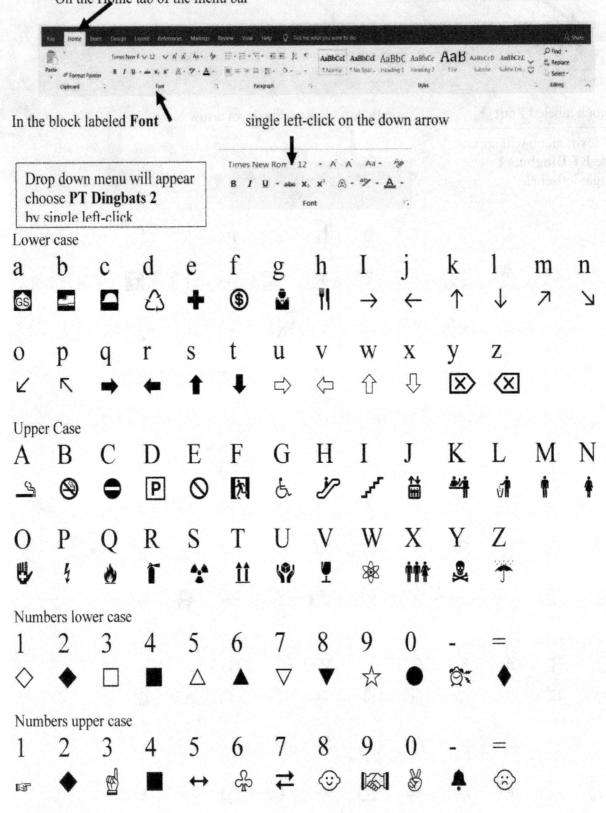

In the block labeled **Font**   single left-click on the down arrow

Drop down menu will appear
choose **PT Dingbats 2**
by single left-click

Lower case

| a | b | c | d | e | f | g | h | I | j | k | l | m | n |

Upper Case

| A | B | C | D | E | F | G | H | I | J | K | L | M | N |

| O | P | Q | R | S | T | U | V | W | X | Y | Z |

Numbers lower case

| 1 | 2 | 3 | 4 | 5 | 6 | 7 | 8 | 9 | 0 | - | = |

Numbers upper case

| 1 | 2 | 3 | 4 | 5 | 6 | 7 | 8 | 9 | 0 | - | = |

Shapes ST

To use these codes, it is necessary to input **Shapes ST** in the font block
On the Home tab of the menu bar

In the block labeled **Font**   single left-click on the down arrow

Drop down menu will appear
choose **Shapes ST**
by single left-click

Lower case

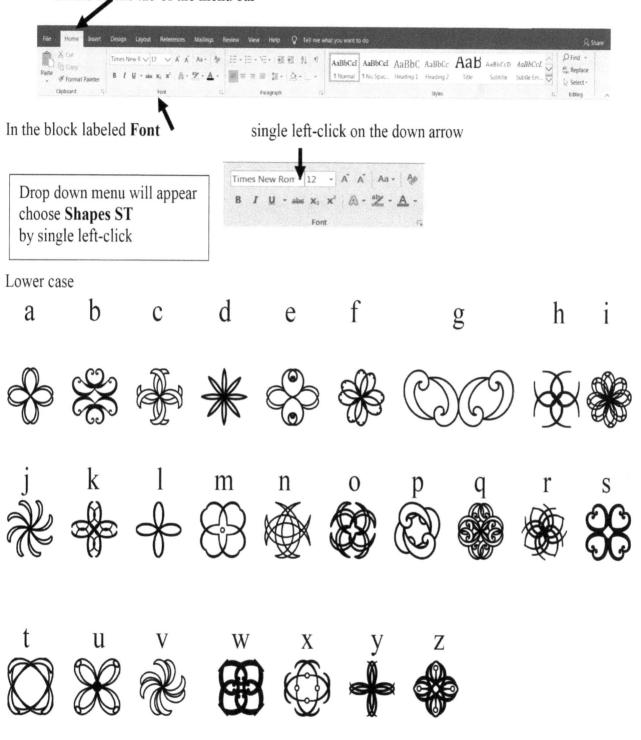

Upper Case letters and numbers identical

Webdings

To use these codes, it is necessary to input **Webdings** in the font block
On the Home tab of the menu bar

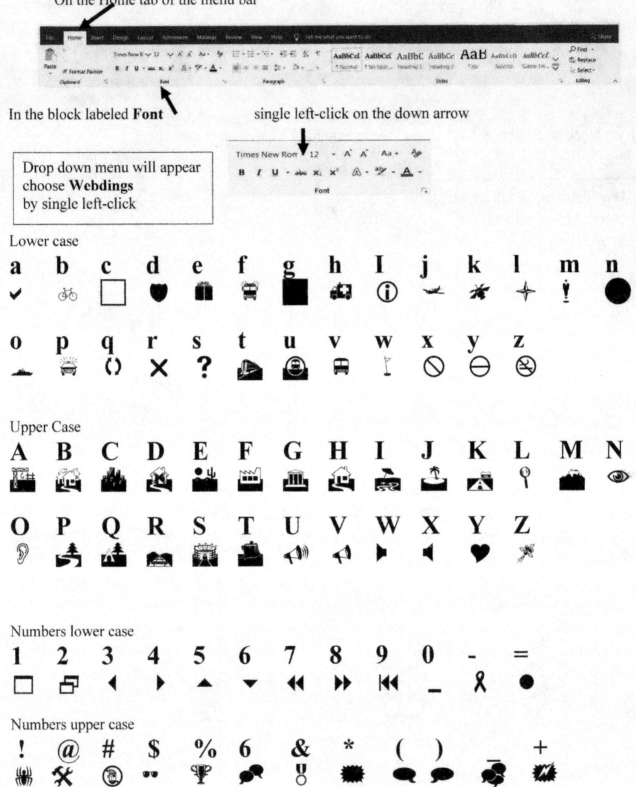

In the block labeled **Font**

single left-click on the down arrow

Drop down menu will appear
choose **Webdings**
by single left-click

Lower case

a b c d e f g h I j k l m n

o p q r s t u v w x y z

Upper Case

A B C D E F G H I J K L M N

O P Q R S T U V W X Y Z

Numbers lower case

1 2 3 4 5 6 7 8 9 0 - =

Numbers upper case

! @ # $ % 6 & * ( ) +

130

Wingdings

To use these codes, it is necessary to input **Wingdings** in the font block
On the Home tab of the menu bar

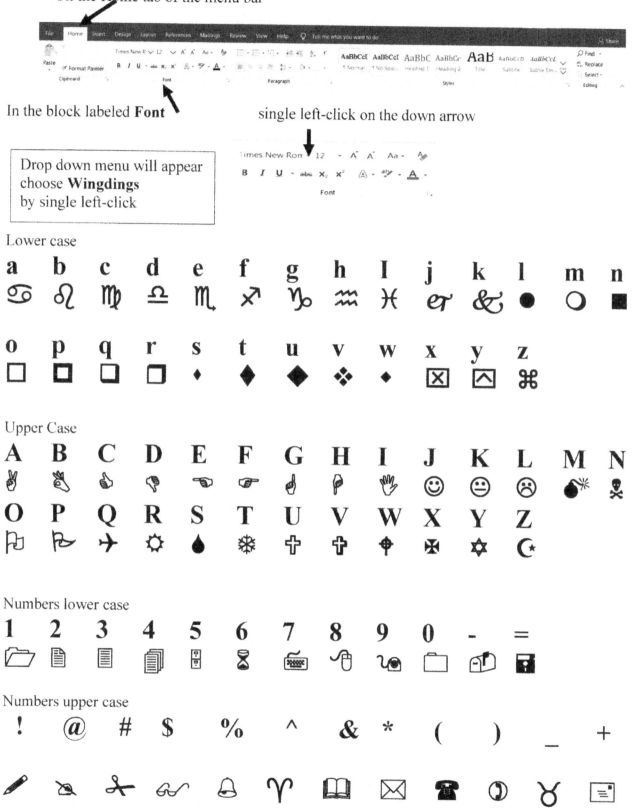

In the block labeled **Font**

single left-click on the down arrow

Drop down menu will appear
choose **Wingdings**
by single left-click

Lower case

a	b	c	d	e	f	g	h	I	j	k	l	m	n

o	p	q	r	s	t	u	v	w	x	y	z

Upper Case

A	B	C	D	E	F	G	H	I	J	K	L	M	N

O	P	Q	R	S	T	U	V	W	X	Y	Z

Numbers lower case

1	2	3	4	5	6	7	8	9	0	-	=

Numbers upper case

!	@	#	$	%	^	&	*	(	)	_	+

Wingdings 2

To use these codes, it is necessary to input **Wingdings 2** in the font block
On the Home tab of the menu bar

In the block labeled **Font**   single left-click on the down arrow

Drop down menu will appear
choose **Wingdings 2**
by single left-click

Lower case

a	b	c	d	e	f	g	h	i	j	k	l	m	n
ℭ	ℬ	ℬ	ℛ	⑨	∿	∿	∿	⓪	①	②	③	④	⑤

o	p	q	r	s	t	u	v	w	x	y	z
☐	☐	☐	☐	◆	◆	◆	❖	◆	⊠	△	⌘

Upper Case

A	B	C	D	E	F	G	H	I	J	K	L	M	N
☜	☞	☞	☛	☚	✋	✋	☝	☝	☟	☝	☟	☟	✋

O	P	Q	R	S	T	U	V	W	X	Y	Z
✗	✓	☒	☑	☒	☒	⊗	⊗	⊘	⊘	ℯ	&

Numbers lower case

1	2	3	4	5	6	7	8	9	0	-	=
🗐	🗒	🗑	🗖	▢	🖶	🖷	⊙	🖸	▢	🗎	♍

Numbers upper case

!	@	#	$	%	^	&	*	(	)	_	+
✒	☚	🖊	🖊	✂	❓	✂	☐	⟩	🗎	❔	🗐

Wingdings 3

To use these codes, it is necessary to input **Wingdings 3** in the font block
On the Home tab of the menu bar

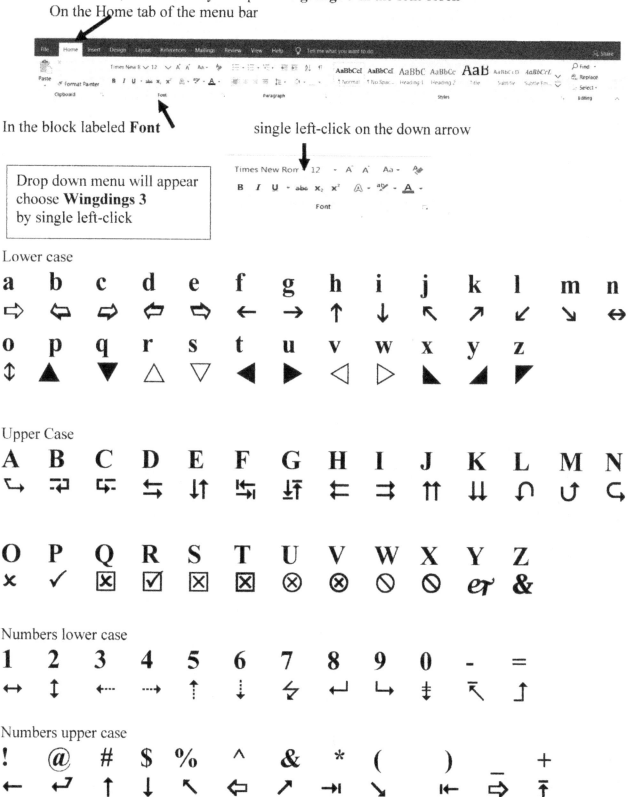

In the block labeled **Font**

single left-click on the down arrow

Drop down menu will appear
choose **Wingdings 3**
by single left-click

Lower case

a	b	c	d	e	f	g	h	i	j	k	l	m	n
⇨	⇦	⇨	⇦	⇨	←	→	↑	↓	↖	↗	↙	↘	↔

o	p	q	r	s	t	u	v	w	x	y	z
↕	▲	▼	△	▽	◄	►	◁	▷	◣	◢	◥

Upper Case

A	B	C	D	E	F	G	H	I	J	K	L	M	N
↳	↴	⇥	⇄	↕	↯	↧	⇤	⇥	⇈	⇊	∩	↻	↺

O	P	Q	R	S	T	U	V	W	X	Y	Z
✗	✓	☒	☑	☒	☒	⊗	⊗	⊘	⊘	ℰ	&

Numbers lower case

1	2	3	4	5	6	7	8	9	0	-	=
↔	↕	←··	··→	↑	↓	↯	↵	↳	‡	↖	↑

Numbers upper case

!	@	#	$	%	^	&	*	(	)	_	+
←	↵	↑	↓	↖	⇦	↗	→|	↘	↤	⇨	↥

Alt Symbol Codes

To use these codes, it is necessary to <u>press and hold</u> **Alt** key, then input the number keys

☺	1		§	21		)	41
☻	2		▬	22		*	42
♥	3		↕	23		+	43
♦	4		↑	24		,	44
♣	5		↓	25		-	45
♠	6		→	26		.	46
•	7		←	27		/	47
▫	8		∟	28		0	48
○	9		↔	29		1	49
◎	10		▲	30		2	50
♂	11		▼	31		3	51
♀	12		space	32		4	52
♪	13		!	33		5	53
♫	14		"	34		6	54
☼	15		#	35		7	55
►	16		$	36		8	56
◄	17		%	37		9	57
↕	18		&	38		:	58
‼	19		'	39		;	59
¶	20		(	40		<	60

=	61	T	84	k	107
>	62	U	85	l	108
?	63	V	86	m	109
@	64	W	87	n	110
A	65	X	88	o	111
B	66	Y	89	p	112
C	67	Z	90	q	113
D	68	[	91	r	114
E	69	\	92	s	115
F	70	]	93	t	116
G	71	^	94	u	117
H	72	_	95	v	118
I	73	`	96	w	119
J	74	a	97	x	120
K	75	b	98	y	121
L	76	c	99	z	122
M	77	d	100	{	123
N	78	e	101	|	124
O	79	f	102	}	125
P	80	g	103		
Q	81	h	104	~	126
R	82	i	105	⌂	127
S	83	j	106	Ç	128
				ü	129

é	130	Ö	153	▒	176
â	131	Ü	154	▓	177
ä	132	¢	155	█	178
à	133	£	156	│	179
å	134	¥	157	┤	180
ç	135	Pts	158	╡	181
ê	136	ƒ	159	╢	182
ë	137	á	160	╖	183
è	138	í	161	╕	184
ï	139	ó	162	╣	185
î	140	ú	163	║	186
ì	141	ñ	164	╗	187
Ä	142	Ñ	165	╝	188
Å	143	ª	166	╜	189
É	144	º	167	╛	190
æ	145	¿	168	┐	191
Æ	146	⌐	169	└	192
ô	147	¬	170	┴	193
ö	148	½	171	┬	194
ò	149	¼	172	├	195
û	150	¡	173	─	196
ù	151	«	174	┼	197
ÿ	152	»	175	╞	198

Symbol	Code	Symbol	Code
╟	199	▌	222
╚	200	▄	223
╔	201	α	224
╩	202	ß	225
╦	203	Γ	226
╠	204	π	227
═	205	Σ	228
╬	206	σ	229
╧	207	μ	230
╨	208	τ	231
╤	209	Φ	232
╥	210	Θ	233
╙	211	Ω	234
╘	212	δ	235
╒	213	∞	236
╓	214	φ	237
╫	215	ε	238
╪	216	∩	239
┘	217	≡	240
┌	218	±	241
█	219		242
▄	220	≤	243
▐	221	⌠	244

137

Text Boxes

What: A text boxes provides a method of accentuating text and positioning it appropriately within your document

Why: A text box provides a method of emphasizing content and helps the reader to identify important information. Microsoft Word provides a way to format and draw your own text block. Additionally, a variety of preformatted text boxes are available.

How: **Inserting a Hand-Drawn Text Box**

On the menu bar choose the **Insert**

menu will change

choose **Text Box** single left-click

menu will change

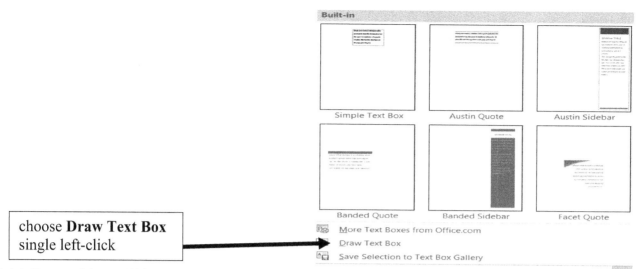

choose **Draw Text Box**
single left-click

Initially, nothing will happen until you move your cursor into the document

Then the screen will change and a $+$ symbol will appear

This will mark the location of the text box

Left click and hold the button down and scroll to create desired size of text box

Release the mouse button

The text box will appear

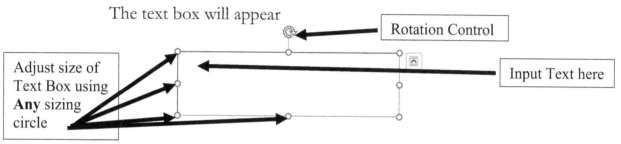

Rotation Control

Input Text here

Adjust size of Text Box using **Any** sizing circle

Single left-click   text box is complete

To Relocate the Text Box

Place the cursor **I** near the edge of the of the text box it will change to

Press the left button on the mouse and hold it down

Drag the box to the new location by scrolling

Release the left button

Box is now relocated

Should the need arise to remove the text box and its contents

Highlight it

depress Delete **m** key on keyboard

Inserting a Preformatted Text Box

On the menu bar choose the **Insert**

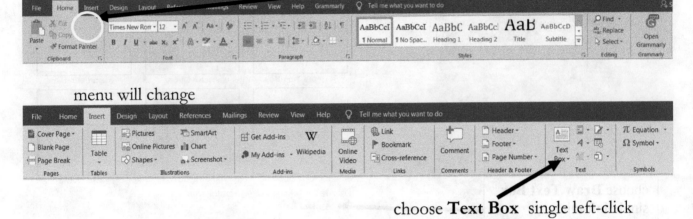

menu will change

choose **Text Box** single left-click

menu will change

Choose desired Box

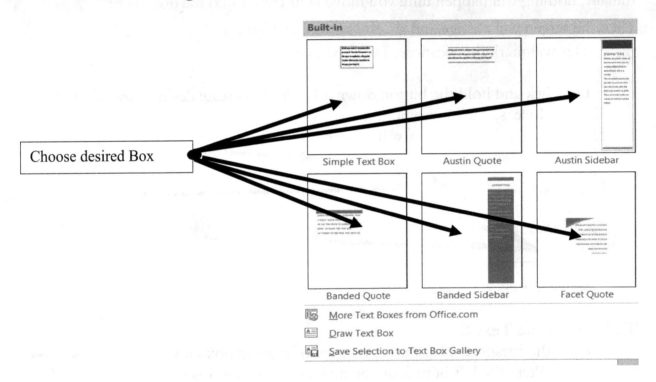

Selected box will appear

[Grab your reader's attention with a great quote from the document or use this space to emphasize a key point. To place this text box anywhere on the page, just drag it.]

Please cursor in box with highlighted preinstalled text
>> Press delete key on keyboard   text will disappear
>>>> Input desired text
>>>>> The text box can now be edited for size and shape as needed

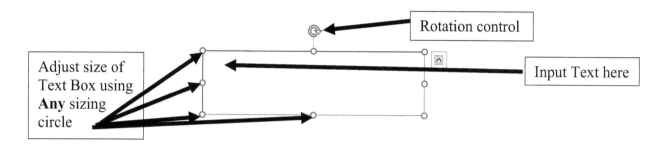

To Relocate the Preformatted Text Box

Place the cursor I near the edge of the of the text box   it will change to
Press the left button on the mouse and hold it down
Drag the box to the new location by scrolling
Release the left button
Box is now relocated

Should the need arise to remove the text box
Double left-click on text box to highlight it
Click on the Delete key

There are many more options available for working with text boxes
When a text box has been selected
A new menu bar will appear

These functions are similar to those used in inserting shapes or symbols
(see snippets   Inserting a Shape)

Text Wrapping

What: Text wrap is a <u>feature</u> that enables you to surround a picture or diagram with <u>text</u>. The text wraps around the graphic.

Why: Wrapping text around figures, can give your documents a more polished look and help focus attention on the content.

How: Text wrapping comes into play when images and text are integrated in a document.

On the Home tab of the menu bar
      choose the **Insert** tab   single left-click

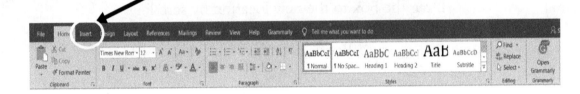

menu will change

Choose **Pictures**   highlight and single left-click
      Choose a picture from your picture library and click on **Insert**

Picture will appear in your document at cursor location

On the **Layout** tab of the menu bar   single left-click

menu will change

Highlight and single left-click **Wrap Text**

Menu will change to display different options for wrapping text

- ⌐ In Line with Text
- ⌐ Square
- ⌐ Tight
- ⌐ Through
- ⌐ Top and Bottom
- ⌐ Behind Text
- ⌐ In Front of Text
- ⌐ Edit Wrap Points
- ✓ Move with Text
- Fix Position on Page
- ⊓ More Layout Options...

It is possible to combine the image with text in different ways

Example: **In Line with Text**

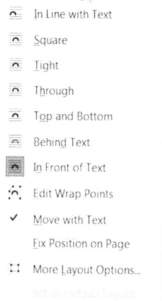

Lorem ipsum dolor sit amet, consectetur adipiscing elit. Fusce quis ante metus. In vitae molestie lacus, vitae facilisis dui. Mauris lobortis imperdiet enim vel posuere. Etiam id scelerisque orci. Etiam pellentesque pretium feugiat. Pellentesque libero turpis, rhoncus ut risus imperdiet, rutrum hendrerit risus. In imperdiet elit ac diam cursus convallis. Sed mattis, odio id scelerisque aliquam, quam velit interdum erat, eu suscipit augue nunc at ex. Nam vitae eros sed eros luctus scelerisque.

Square Lorem ipsum Fusce quis ante metus. In lobortis imperdiet enim pellentesque pretium risus imperdiet, rutrum  dolor sit amet, consectetur adipiscing elit. vitae molestie lacus, vitae facilisis dui. Mauris vel posuere. Etiam id scelerisque orci. Etiam feugiat. Pellentesque libero turpis, rhoncus ut hendrerit risus. In imperdiet elit ac diam cursus convallis. Sed mattis, odio id scelerisque aliquam, quam velit interdum erat, eu suscipit augue nunc at ex. Nam vitae eros sed eros luctus scelerisque.

Tight

Lorem ipsum dolor sit  amet, consectetur adipiscing elit. Fusce quis ante metus. In vitae lobortis imperdiet enim pellentesque pretium risus imperdiet, rutrum cursus convallis. Sed mattis, odio id scelerisque aliquam, quam velit interdum erat, eu suscipit augue nunc at ex. Nam vitae eros sed eros luctus scelerisque.

molestie lacus, vitae facilisis dui. Mauris vel posuere. Etiam id scelerisque orci. Etiam feugiat. Pellentesque libero turpis, rhoncus ut hendrerit risus. In imperdiet elit ac diam

Top and Bottom

Lorem ipsum dolor sit amet, consectetur adipiscing elit. Fusce quis ante metus. In vitae molestie lacus, vitae 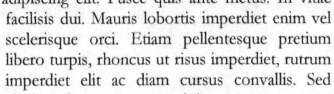 facilisis dui. Mauris lobortis imperdiet enim vel posuere. Etiam id feugiat. Pellentesque hendrerit risus. In scelerisque orci. Etiam pellentesque pretium libero turpis, rhoncus ut risus imperdiet, rutrum imperdiet elit ac diam cursus convallis. Sed mattis, odio id scelerisque aliquam, quam velit interdum erat, eu suscipit augue nunc at ex. Nam vitae eros sed eros luctus scelerisque.

Move with text   If the **Move with Text** option is selected in **Wrap text**

It is possible to point and drag the image to any point in the text

Insert picture or shape in document at any point

Click on picture or shape and hold left button down

Drag to new location

Examples:

Lorem ipsum dolor sit amet, consectetur adipiscing elit. Fusce quis ante metus. In vitae molestie lacus, vitae facilisis dui. Mauris lobortis imperdiet enim vel posuere. Etiam id scelerisque orci. Etiam pellentesque pretium feugiat. Pellentesque libero turpis, rhoncus ut risus imperdiet, rutrum hendrerit risus. In imperdiet elit ac diam cursus convallis. Sed mattis, odio id scelerisque aliquam, quam velit interdum erat, eu suscipit augue nunc at ex. Nam vitae eros sed eros luctus scelerisque.

Lorem ipsum dolor sit amet, consectetur adipiscing elit. Fusce quis ante metus. In vitae molestie lacus, vitae facilisis dui. Mauris lobortis imperdiet enim vel posuere. Etiam id scelerisque orci. Etiam pellentesque pretium feugiat. Pellentesque libero turpis, rhoncus ut risus imperdiet, rutrum hendrerit risus. In imperdiet elit ac diam cursus convallis. Sed mattis, odio id scelerisque aliquam, quam velit interdum erat, eu suscipit augue nunc at ex. Nam vitae eros sed eros luctus scelerisque.

Lorem ipsum dolor sit amet, consectetur adipiscing elit. Fusce quis ante metus. In vitae molestie lacus, vitae  facilisis dui. Mauris lobortis imperdiet enim vel posuere. Etiam id scelerisque orci. Etiam pellentesque pretium feugiat. Pellentesque libero turpis, rhoncus ut risus imperdiet, rutrum hendrerit risus. In imperdiet elit ac diam cursus convallis. Sed mattis, odio id scelerisque aliquam, quam velit interdum erat, eu suscipit augue nunc at ex. Nam vitae eros sed eros luctus scelerisque.

Lorem ipsum dolor sit amet, consectetur adipiscing elit. Fusce quis ante metus. In vitae molestie lacus, vitae facilisis dui. Mauris lobortis imperdiet enim vel posuere. Etiam id scelerisque orci. Etiam pellentesque pretium feugiat. Pellentesque libero turpis, rhoncus ut risus imperdiet, rutrum hendrerit risus. In imperdiet elit ac diam cursus convallis. Sed mattis, odio id scelerisque aliquam, quam velit interdum erat, eu suscipit augue nunc at ex. Nam vitae eros sed eros luctus scelerisque.

Release mouse button to place graphic in text

Understanding Fonts

What: Fonts are text characters using different forms of letters. Examples: ABC, ABC, 𝔄𝔅ℭ. A graphical representation of text in a different typeface, Microsoft Word offers a vast selection of fonts. Others can be added. The size of the letters is determined by the font size. The higher the number, the larger the letter.

Why: Different fonts provide a means of adding emphasis and clarity to a document. The type of font used is determined by the information you are presenting. Times New Roman 12, is an often used font in documents.

How: When using Microsoft Word, changing the font, the characteristics of the font and the size are easily managed.

Single left-click on the **Home** tab

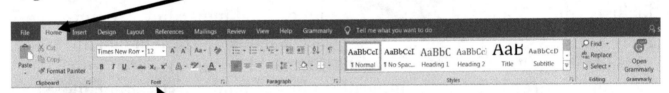

in the block labeled **Font**.

Single left-click on the down arrow in the block labeled Times New Roman

A drop-down menu will appear which will display available fonts.

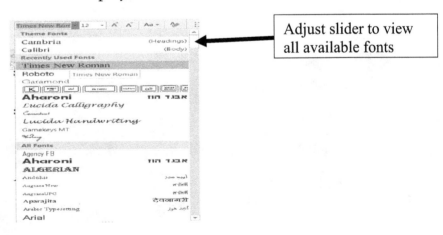

Adjust slider to view all available fonts

To choose a font from the listing.

Single left-click on it

> The name of this font will now appear in the block which previously listed Times New Roman.
>
>> Your document will now display this font.

Changing the size of the font.

There are different ways to change the size of the font:

One) Single left-click on the number.

> The number will be highlighted.
>
>> Using the keyboard input the desired size using numerical keys. (The higher the number, the larger the font)

Two) Single left-click on the down arrow

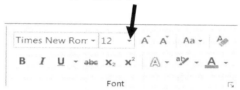

> A drop-down menu will appear which displays a list of numbers. Highlight desired number, then single left-click

Three) To the right of the font size block are two indicators for increasing or decreasing font size

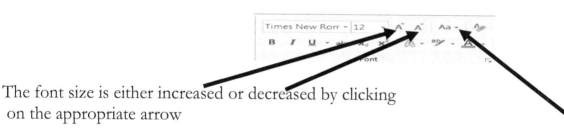

The font size is either increased or decreased by clicking on the appropriate arrow

Four) It is possible to change the <u>case of the font</u> by single left-clicking

a menu will appear

Undo Function

What: The Undo command undoes the last action taken. Deletes last item input. Each click on this icon provides a means of stepping backward through the document. Extremely useful.

Why: Mistakes happen because learning is a complicated process.

How: There are two different methods of using the undo function

           Method 1   Using Keyboard Keys

           Method 2   Using Quick Access Toolbar

Method 1   Using Keyboard Keys for Undo

Press **Control** and **Z** simultaneously (**v Z**)

    Removes last action

        Each time these keys combination are pressed

        You step back one step

Method 2 Using the Quick Access Toolbar

On the menu bar   is the Quick Access Toolbar

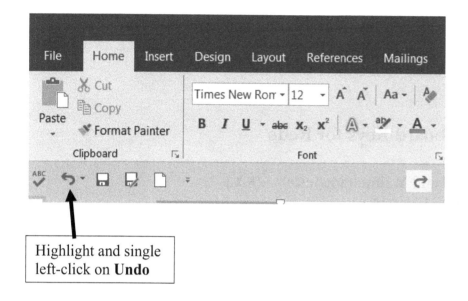

Highlight and single
left-click on **Undo**

Each time this icon is single left-clicked

The last action is undone

This can be done repeatedly to step backward in the document

If this icon is not located in the quick access toolbar, it can easily be added

In the section labeled **Snippets**

Follow instructions for creating icons in the **Quick Access Toolbar**

Redo Function

What: The Redo command restores the last item deleted. Extremely useful.

Why: Mistakes happen.

How: There are two different methods of using the undo function
           Method 1   Using Keyboard Keys
           Method 2   Using Quick Access Toolbar

Method 1 Using Keyboard Keys for Redo

Press **Control** and **Y** simultaneously   **(vY)**
       Reverses last action

Method 2 Using the Quick Access Toolbar

On the menu bar   choose Quick Access Toolbar

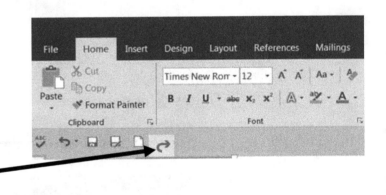

Highlight and single left-click **Redo**

When this icon is single left-clicked
The previous Undo action is reversed

If this icon is not located in the quick access toolbar, it can easily be added
In the section labeled **Snippets: Quick Action Toolbar**
Follow instructions for creating Quick Access Toolbar and Icons

Spellchecker

What: Spell check is a software program that corrects spelling errors in word processing document. It checks, identifies and corrects misspelled words. Be careful, remember this is only a machine and machines do make mistakes.

Why: Spelling is a complicated process and requires careful editing.

How: There are three main methods to initiate the spellchecker
         1) **Keyboard** method
         2) **Utilizing the Review tab**
         3) **Utilizing the Quick Access Toolbar**

Method 1 Keyboard Method
On the keyboard press the **F7** key

menu will change
and display your document and identify any perceived errors by highlighting them

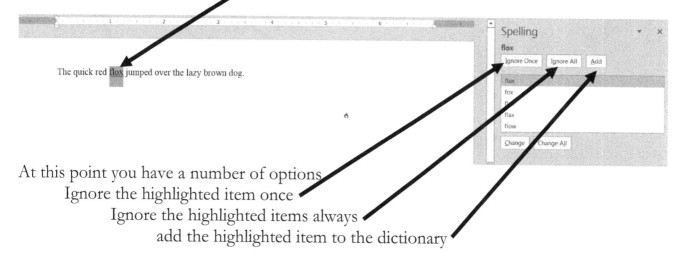

At this point you have a number of options
     Ignore the highlighted item once
         Ignore the highlighted items always
            add the highlighted item to the dictionary

highlight the correct spelling of the word in the white block (fox)
and single left-click on it

your document will allow display the word you selected

Method 2   Utilizing the Review Tab

On the Home tab menu bar

choose the **Review** tab   single left-click

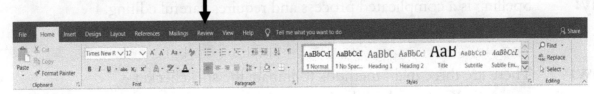

menu will change

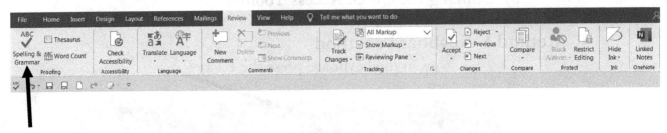

choose **Spelling and Grammar**   single left-click

The menu will change and display your document
and identify any perceived errors by highlighting

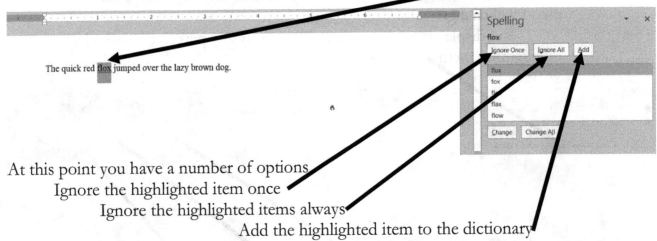

At this point you have a number of options
Ignore the highlighted item once
Ignore the highlighted items always
Add the highlighted item to the dictionary
highlight the correct spelling of the word in the
white block (fox) and single left-click on it
your document will now display the word you selected

Method 3   Utilizing the Quick Access Toolbar

On the menu bar   choose the **Quick Action Toolbar**

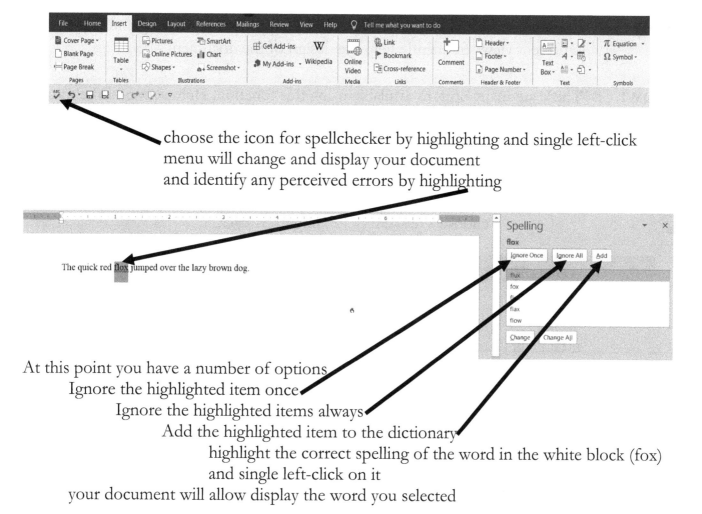

choose the icon for spellchecker by highlighting and single left-click
menu will change and display your document
and identify any perceived errors by highlighting

At this point you have a number of options
        Ignore the highlighted item once
                Ignore the highlighted items always
                    Add the highlighted item to the dictionary
                        highlight the correct spelling of the word in the white block (fox)
                        and single left-click on it
        your document will allow display the word you selected

(Go to the section labeled snippets and then follow instructions on how to create, add, delete icons on the Quick Access Toolbar)

Using View

What: This function allows the document be viewed in different ways and formats

Why: Certain documents may require a different approach to viewing and editing. Different views frequently help the design of the document

How: There are many options available using this function. Here is one of the most useful

On the **Home** tab of the Menu Bar
           choose **View** tab   single left-click

menu will change

Expanded **View** section of toolbar

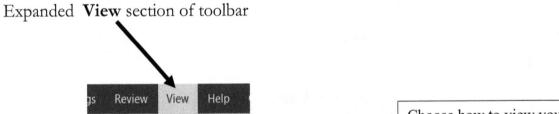

Choose how to view your document
Highlight and single left-click to select

Additional Options   Viewing more than one page at a time:
(useful when editing format of large document)

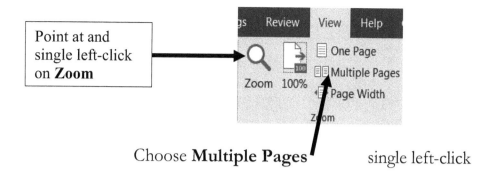

Point at and single left-click on **Zoom**

Choose **Multiple Pages**   single left-click

menu will change

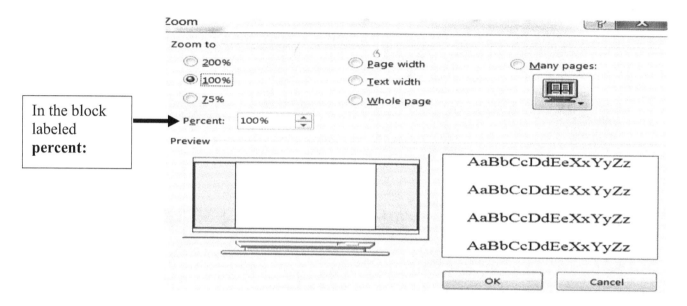

In the block labeled **percent:**

Changing the percentages in this block will change the number of pages per row

10% equals	11 pages per row
15% equals	8 pages per row
20% equals	6 pages per row
30% equals	4 pages per row
40% equals	3 pages per row
50% equals	2 pages per row

Special note:

It is possible to <u>increase or decrease</u> the size of the pages you're working on by using your mouse or trackball. Press and hold down the Control key and then <u>scroll up or down</u> using the <u>scrolling wheel</u> on the mouse

Watermarks

What: Watermarks are a faint design made over a printed document. The intensity and the color are adjustable.

Why: At times it is beneficial to identify a document as a draft or confidential document.

How: Open the document in which you wish to insert a Watermark

On the **Home** tab of the menu bar
choose **Design** tab   single left-click

menu will change

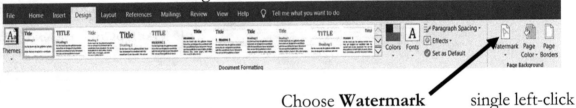

Choose **Watermark**   single left-click

menu will change

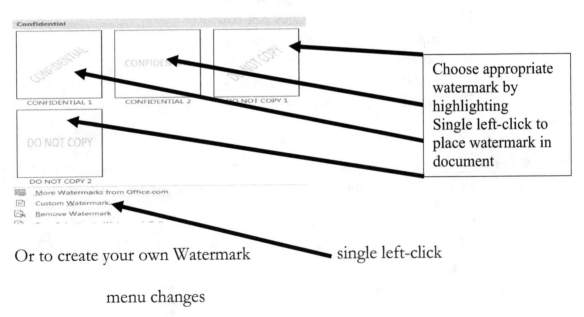

Choose appropriate watermark by highlighting
Single left-click to place watermark in document

Or to create your own Watermark   single left-click

menu changes

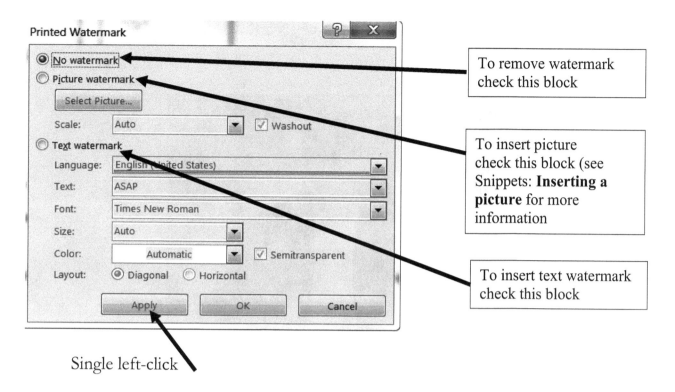

Printed Watermark

- ◉ No watermark → To remove watermark check this block
- ○ Picture watermark
  - Select Picture...
  - Scale: Auto ▾ ☑ Washout
- ○ Text watermark
  - Language: English (United States) ▾
  - Text: ASAP ▾
  - Font: Times New Roman ▾
  - Size: Auto ▾
  - Color: Automatic ▾ ☑ Semitransparent
  - Layout: ◉ Diagonal ○ Horizontal

Apply OK Cancel

To insert picture check this block (see Snippets: **Inserting a picture** for more information

To insert text watermark check this block

Single left-click

Watermark will appear on all pages of document

About the Author

Born on the shores of Lake Michigan. Educated in Waukegan, Illinois and at University of Hawaii: BAs in Psychology and Communication, MA Communications. Graduate work in Educational Communications.

Eight books published. Recipient of more than 100 writing awards for prose and poetry. Guest speaker at various organizations in area. Currently, President of Twin Lakes Writers in Mountain Home Arkansas, and Chair the Hardy Writers

.

Fourteen years in the U.S. Air Force: Weapons Specialist, Supervisory Electronic Communications Specialist. NRA Lifetime Master-Pistol, indoor and outdoor, with three guns (.22, Centerfire, .45). Served in Federal Government: Internal Revenue Service and Department of Labor.

Married with three children, five grandchildren. Living in the Ozark Mountains at The Thinking Rocks.

Index